AGE
OF EXPLORATION

GREAT AGES OF MAN

A History of the World's Cultures

AGE
OF EXPLORATION

by

JOHN R. HALE

and

The Editors of TIME-LIFE Books

TIME INCORPORATED, NEW YORK

TIME-LIFE BOOKS

FOUNDER: Henry R. Luce 1898-1967

Editor-in-Chief: Hedley Donovan
Chairman of the Board: Andrew Heiskell
President: James R. Shepley

Vice Chairman: Roy E. Larsen

MANAGING EDITOR: Jerry Korn
Assistant Managing Editors: Ezra Bowen,
David Maness, Martin Mann, A. B. C. Whipple
Planning Director: Oliver E. Allen
Art Director: Sheldon Cotler
Chief of Research: Beatrice T. Dobie
Director of Photography: Melvin L. Scott
Senior Text Editors: Diana Hirsh, William Frankel
Assistant Planning Director: Carlotta Kerwin
Assistant Art Director: Arnold C. Holeywell
Assistant Chief of Research: Myra Mangan

PUBLISHER: Joan D. Manley
General Manager: John D. McSweeney
Business Manager: John Steven Maxwell
Sales Director: Carl G. Jaeger
Promotion Director: Paul R. Stewart
Public Relations Director: Nicholas Benton

GREAT AGES OF MAN
Editorial Staff for *Age of Exploration:*
EDITOR: Russell Bourne
Assistant Editor: Carlotta Kerwin
Text Editor: Ogden Tanner
Picture Editor: Isabelle Rubin
Designer: Norman Snyder
Assistant Designer: Ladislav Svatos
Staff Writers: Sam Halper, Peter Meyerson,
Lucille Schulberg, John von Hartz
Chief Researcher: Nancy Shuker
Picture Research: Harriet Delihas
Text Research: Susan Apple, Barbara Ballantine,
Terry Drucker, Lea Guyer, Helen Isaacs,
Carol Isenberg, Jeffrey Tarter, Rachel Tyrrell,
Linda Wolfe

EDITORIAL PRODUCTION
Production Editor: Douglas B. Graham
Assistant Production Editors:
Gennaro C. Esposito, Feliciano Madrid
Quality Director: Robert L. Young
Assistant Quality Director: James J. Cox
Associate: Serafino J. Cambareri
Copy Staff: Eleanore W. Karsten (chief),
Rosalind Stubenberg, Florence Keith, Pearl Sverdlin
Picture Department: Dolores A. Littles,
Barbara Sullivan
Art Assistants: Anne Landry, Robert Pellegrini
Traffic: Carmen McLellan

THE AUTHOR: John R. Hale is Professor of Italian at University College, London. Formerly a Fellow and Tutor at Jesus College, Oxford, he has served as chairman of the Department of History at the University of Warwick in England and has also taught at Cornell University. His publications include *England and the Italian Renaissance, Machiavelli and Renaissance Italy, The Evolution of British Historiography* and *Renaissance,* another volume in the Great Ages of Man series.

THE CONSULTING EDITOR: Leonard Krieger, University Professor of History at the University of Chicago, was formerly Professor of History at Yale and Columbia universities. Dr. Krieger is the author of *The German Idea of Freedom* and *The Politics of Discretion,* and is co-author of *History,* written in collaboration with John Higham and Felix Gilbert.

THE COVER: An embellished map, drawn by the French navigator-cartographer Guillaume le Testu in 1556, shows the Cape of Good Hope above a misplaced Australia.

Valuable aid in the preparation of this book was given by the following departments and individuals of Time Inc.: photographers Fritz Goro and Leonard McCombe; Editorial Production, Norman Airey; Library, Benjamin Lightman; Picture Collection, Doris O'Neil; Photographic Laboratory, George Karas; TIME-LIFE News Service, Murray J. Gart; Correspondents Maria Vincenza Aloisi (Paris), Barbara Moir and Katharine Sachs (London), Ann Natanson (Rome), Elisabeth Kraemer (Bonn), Jean Bratton (Madrid), Friso Endt (Amsterdam), Marvine Howe (Lisbon), Jerrold Schecter (Tokyo) and Traudl Lessing (Vienna).

CONTENTS

INTRODUCTION

Between 1420 and 1620 Europeans learned that all seas are one; that seamen, given adequate ships and stores, skill and courage, could in time reach any country in the world which had an ocean coast, and—what was more important—return home. No other period in the history of the Western world equals this time in significance, in variety and in dramatic interest. Not the least important of its by-products was the demolition of geographical theories that had prevailed in Europe since classical antiquity. Nowhere in the writings of Ptolemy, for example, was there any hint of the immense American continent or of the vast Pacific Ocean.

Today, when the world is on the brink of the exploration of space, we have new reasons for wishing to understand the motives, the means and the achievements of the old discoverers. This is not easy, for their story, so familiar in general outline, is hard to follow in detail. There are very few eyewitness accounts of major voyages, and fewer still written by leaders of expeditions. The reports of Vasco da Gama, of Ferdinand Magellan, of Sebastián del Cano, have disappeared. Columbus' journal survives, but only in an abstract made by another hand; and even so it describes as much what Columbus wished to see as what he actually saw. Most explorers were practical men, little given to writing. They saw no reason to give away valuable information, except to their employers. The employers encouraged this taciturnity, because they hoped to monopolize the profits of the new-found lands. The details of discovery, therefore, have often to be inferred from the writings of chroniclers and armchair amateurs of travel, which were based upon classical theory and cosmographical conjecture as well as upon experience.

The Age of Exploration is commonly associated with the Renaissance; with a quickening of curiosity, with a new clarity and detachment in studying natural phenomena and human achievement. Yet there was nothing new about travel, about the desire to see strange lands. What *was* new was the systematic organization of maritime reconnaissance and the rapid improvement in its techniques. Once rulers and financiers understood that more efficient ships, more accurate instruments and better methods of cartography and navigation had made long ocean passages possible, they invested in exploring. Their object was not discovery for its own sake— that was incidental—but the opening of ocean routes to distant India, China and Japan, countries known to exist and believed to be of commercial importance. The men who did the work were tough professionals, willing to serve any ruler who would employ them, ready to go anywhere and investigate anything if they were suitably rewarded. They were the maritime counterparts of the mercenary captains who made a profession of the land fighting of Europe. Skillful, imaginative and bold, they drew the map of the world we know.

So dramatic and so complex a tale is best told plainly; it needs no hyperbole. Professor Hale relates and analyzes the story of the discoverers in clear, unsentimental prose, not belittling their courage, their vision and their faith but properly emphasizing the systematic purpose which drove them, the inventiveness, the technical ingenuity and the judgment which made possible their success.

J. H. PARRY
Gardiner Professor of Oceanic History and Affairs
Harvard University

A
Concept of the World
during the
Age of Exploration

Legend, Dream & Fact

The "Northwest Passage"

Mythical Islands
of the Atlantic

The Elusive
Seven Cities of Cibola

The Fabled
Fountain of Youth

The Dream of
Terrestrial Paradise

"El Dorado"
— the Gilded Man

A Fearsome
Patagonian
Giant

David Greenspan

The "Northeast Passage"

The Treasure Houses
of Cathay

Headless Men

The Missionary
Apostle
St. Thomas

The Priest-King
Prester John

The Legendary
Southern Continent,
"Terra Australis Incognita"

After the World Map of Gerhardus Mercator–Duisburg, 1569

1
THE EVE
OF ADVENTURE

The Renaissance voyages of discovery rank as one of history's two or three most important phenomena in terms of their effect on the modern world. In roughly two centuries, from about 1420 to 1620, the urge to find new lands beyond Europe led to an unprecedented increase in knowledge about this planet. Discovery led to colonization and settlement, to overseas commitments that influenced the rise and fall of nations in Europe. It brought new wealth, new products, new opportunities, new problems, new ways of thinking. It led to the creation of new nations, the United States among them.

The exploits of the men whose names evoke the Age of Exploration—Vasco da Gama, Christopher Columbus, Ferdinand Magellan and many others —have become so familiar that it rarely occurs to anyone to ask the obvious questions about them. Why did the great discoveries coincide with the Renaissance, instead of occurring (for example) in the 12th or 13th Centuries? And why did the initiative come from western Europe? Why not from one of several other relatively advanced civilizations? China, India and Japan in Asia; Islam in Africa, the Middle East and parts of Europe; the Aztecs, Inca and Maya in the Americas—all of these possessed large territories, great wealth and levels of civilization in some respects equal, if not superior, to those of the European nations. Yet leadership in exploration was taken by Portugal, Spain, England, France and the Netherlands, almost to the exclusion of all other lands.

Two points should be noted at the start. First, it is somewhat misleading to talk about "discovery," for the word implies finding something new, something that has not been known about before. But the peoples of America and Asia knew about their own lands. Moreover, a goodly number of the lands explored during the Renaissance had thriving populations; sometimes they possessed books and maps describing their countries, and this information was gratefully taken over by the European voyagers. So the men who claimed to have "discovered" new lands were using the word as subjectively as the New Yorker who "discovers" San Francisco for the first time.

Second, it must be understood that travel itself was nothing new to Europeans. In the 13th Cen-

THE TERRORS OF THE OCEAN *faced by early explorers are suggested in this painting by Pieter Brueghel. They included violent storms, uncharted horizons and whalelike "sea monsters"—one of which can be glimpsed diving beneath the water at center foreground, oblivious of the barrel that has been tossed overboard (right), presumably to divert it from attacking the ship.*

tury, Giovanni de Plano Carpini, Willem van Rujs-broek and Marco Polo had penetrated deep into Asia. Scandinavians of the Dark Ages preceded Columbus to America. What was novel about the period 1420-1620 was that travel was systematized by governments and merchant companies. From an age of sporadic, largely unsponsored, independent travel, Europe moved to a time of travel with a purpose, of exploration rather than individual globe-trotting. And at no other period have men sailed so far or discovered so widely in so short a time as did the seamen of the Renaissance.

There was a special quality about the needs, the skills, and the imagination of Europeans in this age that sent them searching the globe. Renaissance Europe needed precious metals and spices. While individual merchants had sought for gold and silk, pepper and cloves in the Far East during the Middle Ages, it was only in the 15th Century that governments joined in the search. This was not due merely to greed. Europe was genuinely desperate for metal to make into coin: its own gold deposits, such as those in Ireland, were exhausted, and the silver mines of Germany, though rich, were unable to cope with the demand. Without ample supplies of coin, there could be no real expansion of commercial and financial transactions. Bullion was not just wealth, but the means of obtaining wealth.

Nor were spices then, as they are now, simply a way to add a whiff of individuality to food. Difficulties of transport and a lack of refrigeration meant that most of the meat that Renaissance men ate was salted or spoiled; spices were needed to make food edible, not merely more delicious.

Along with the need for precious metals and spices there was the desire to please God by converting the heathen. The crusading motive was perfectly genuine, though it, too, had its practical side: converted natives were more docile, converted chiefs were more cooperative. This holy zeal also led to

WELCOMED BY NATIVES *on the island of Hispaniola in December 1492, Christopher Columbus and two helmeted aides receive lavish gifts of the gold and gems they hoped to find. A second incentive of the explorers—missionary zeal —is also depicted in this composite tableau, engraved in 1594 by the Flemish artist Theodor de Bry: at left, members of Columbus' crew erect a cross on the Bahamian island of San Salvador, their first landfall in North America.*

a certain belief in a divinely inspired mission. King Manuel I of Portugal, writing to the ruler of Calicut in India, explained that men had always wanted to get to India, but "as long as God did not wish it to take place all the men of past times were unable to accomplish it." But now He did wish it, "and it is now . . . a wrong and injury to God to wish to resist His manifest and known will."

Governments and individuals alike sincerely believed that it was Europe's manifest destiny to convert the infidel. Although Columbus knew that his expedition would be judged in terms of the gold and spices he found, he could write with complete sincerity of "what I conceive to be the principal wish of our most serene King, namely, the conversion of these people to the holy faith of Christ."

God and Mammon worked hand in hand from the outset of Renaissance exploration. The Catholic powers always stressed the double aim. The Protestant powers, having no missionary orders at this time, paid less attention to conversion, but they still professed the same motives. Richard Hakluyt, the principal advocate of increased English activity in America, coupled "the possibility of the enlarging of the dominions of the Queen's Most Excellent Majesty, and consequently of her honour, revenues and of her power" with "the glory of God by planting of religion among those infidels."

There was in the Renaissance no governmental interest in exploration merely for the sake of knowledge. When enough gold and silver and spices had been found, and enough Europeans were stationed in overseas posts to exploit the mines and guard the trade routes, Renaissance governments lost interest in exploring. In 1602, when Pero Fernandes de Queiros was trying to obtain backing at the Spanish court for his great voyage into the Pacific, he found that "some answered me that sufficient lands had been discovered for His Majesty, and that what signified was to . . . settle them, rather than go in search of those I said were new."

None of the material needs that underlay the pressure for exploration could have been satisfied without seaworthy ships, suited to discovery, and skillful mariners. Renaissance Europe, alone among maritime communities of the world, possessed both. Here then, is one explanation of why the impetus for exploration came from the European nations that looked out into the Atlantic.

It is true, of course, that almost anything that will float and that has some sort of sail can travel immense distances. The Norsemen crossed the North Atlantic in the 10th Century in open boats, probably with a single sail. But the Scandinavians were desperately short of space at home and prepared to take almost any risks to find a better living by migrating elsewhere. Explorers of the 15th Century, however, were as anxious to get back to their own countries as they were to leave them, for the chief motive behind their voyages was profit, not settlement, and there was no point in finding a new market or source of wealth if news of it could not be brought home.

The fact is that sailors in other parts of the world *were* making remarkable voyages during the 15th Century. Large outrigger sailing canoes were crossing the Indian Ocean between Madagascar and India, and traveling from one Pacific island to another. But these vessels depended on favorable following winds and known currents; they could not fight into the wind as an explorer's craft had to do.

Another type of vessel found in the Indian Ocean was the Arab dhow. Numbers of these crisscrossed the waters around India, the Red Sea and East Africa. Though able craft, they, too, were unsuited to exploration. Their planks were sewn together with coir, a fiber made from coconut husk, and they carried the triangular lateen sail, still a familiar sight in the East. Sewn planking is weaker on the open sea than nailed, and the huge lateen

sail required a larger crew than the square-rigged sails of European ships, a crucial point when voyages of uncertain duration were embarked upon.

By comparison with these craft, the European ships that were developed in the 15th Century could go anywhere and get back. These vessels resulted from a peculiarly European situation, the existence of two distinct shipbuilding traditions—one producing the stout, broad, square-sailed trader of the North Sea and the Atlantic coast, the other the oared galleys and lateen-rigged coasters of the Mediterranean. *(See picture essay, page 85.)* Increasing trade between northern and southern Europe led to a mingling of types, drawing on the best features of those ships designed to sail in an inland sea and those intended for the open ocean.

European ships were superior in another regard: they were armed both with guns firing fore and aft and with others firing broadside through ports cut in the ship's high sides. As a result, European naval gunnery was amazingly effective. This superior fire-power was essential to large-scale exploration, for governments would not have financed the search for new markets and new trade routes unless they were confident of being able to control them. Moreover, captains did not have to rely on the large crew of rowers needed by a Chinese junk, for example, to ram an opponent with sufficient impact, or on auxiliary soldiers required for grapple-and-boarding tactics. The European ship fought best by standing off and using its cannon. It did not have to see its stores consumed by soldiers; its seamen could fight the ship as well as sail it.

The best ship, however, is no better than the men who guide it. In the course of centuries, the maritime nations of Europe had built up an austere tradition of capable and dedicated seamanship. But the voyages of exploration presented hazards unforeseen even by men who had learned to cope with the troubled waters of the English Channel

Labels on the map: REDH HOLM, MIDELFIORD, MALANGER, EGGE, LOKHELLE, HASEVOG, GILLEFIORD, OSTRAFIORD, SANDER, GIGASVN, DANI, CETE, GALLEA PEREGRINA, QVEDEFIORD, LANGE, SKARTA, ROLLEN, LANGANES TRODANES, DVVANES ANDANES, DOMVS BIRCA, RVST, SCONGEN, XII.P, HECESTHORRENDA CARIBDIS, F, VNDERVAL, D, LOFOT, VAST, GAMBLAVIK, HIC FO FREQ, NYGAVIK, PISCES HVETE DICTI, ROOPEDVM, DIA HELGALA TERRA NOBILIVM, HORVPISCIV CAPITIBVS VTVNTVR LOCO LIGNO, PISCA, STEK, TRONDO

HUGE SEA MONSTERS *lurk offshore and feed on various ships (two-masted square-riggers, a one-masted cog, a galley, a rowboat) that ply the fiord-cut coast of northwestern Norway in this 1539 woodcut map by the Swedish cartographer Olaus Magnus. The whirlpool, or "maelstrom," at center was a less fanciful peril. Fed by racing tides, such turbulent waters were strong enough to sink ships, tear apart drifting trees and drown whales—which, as one explorer observed, made "a pitifull crie" as they were sucked in.*

and the icy seas between Scandinavia and Greenland. Taking the period of discovery as a whole, an expedition member's chances of getting back alive were probably about 50-50, with illness—the result of scurvy and other diseases of malnutrition—accounting for most of the deaths. In addition, there were tempests and unmarked shoals in unknown seas, cannibals and constant uncertainty. Yet expedition after expedition was able to find crewmen, and the question arises: Why did they enlist?

It was not for money: the gold their captains sought would go to the Crown, and on a voyage of discovery there was little chance of loot or a division of prize money from a captured treasure galleon. Nor can the crusading motive have stirred the ordinary seaman, who was illiterate and uninterested in theology.

Since no common seaman left an account of the motives that led him to sign on, we can only guess about them. The pay was frequently somewhat higher than for an ordinary trading voyage in familiar waters, and it was certain, for exploration was soundly backed by a royal treasury or by a group of prosperous merchants. Moreover, all seafaring was hard and dangerous in that age. Voyages as long as any of those of Columbus (if not as chancy) were regularly being made from the North Sea to the Levant. It was an age when the average life expectancy was about 30 years, when even on land life was hard and uncertain; more farmers and tradesmen died of plague than did seamen of scurvy. So to Renaissance sailors the hazards of exploration did not present as lurid a contrast to ordinary life as they do by modern standards.

The men who did enlist for the voyages were by no means perfect. Magellan, Sebastian Cabot and Francis Drake were but a few of the explorers who had trouble with mutineers: Henry Hudson's crew sent him to his death. And there are numerous tales of desertions. Captains had to resort to cajolery, threats and bluff to keep their ships pointing away from home; they faked distances, and they showed the men charts that deliberately omitted islands toward which a sullen crew might have forced the pilots to turn.

Many of the recorded complaints deal not with danger or hardship but with the duration of the voyage, and the questionable chances of ever returning to their families. With this in mind, the Amsterdam merchants gave preference to bachelors for Willem Barents' voyage in search of a northeast passage through the Arctic Ocean to China.

Sustained by no explorer's vision, the crew sometimes fell into despair and refused to work the ship. On Queiros' voyage, one of the sailors "said to the Chief Pilot that he was tired of being always tired, that he would rather die once than many times, and that they might as well shut their eyes and let the ship go to the bottom." Nonetheless, some seamen came back for more. At least one man who sailed with Columbus on his first voyage enlisted for the three that followed.

As for the commanders of the expeditions, the hope of riches might have been one of their motives, but none of the great explorers, even Columbus himself, died a wealthy man. Only the conquistadors and the great administrators who ruled in India for Portugal and in the Americas for Spain died with great fortunes. The trail blazers' reward was in the less tangible form of honor and fame.

The desire for personal glory was, however, one of the driving forces of Renaissance endeavor. Men wished to become famous, renowned for wisdom, for munificent patronage or for valor. In Mexico, Hernando Cortes called on his men to imitate the heroic deeds of the Romans. Cortes' companion and chronicler Bernal Díaz, confronted with the giant causeway leading to Mexico City, recorded the thrilling consciousness that the Spaniards' boldness was of a sort that could not possibly be displayed at home. "We didn't know what to say or whether it was real, with all the cities on the land and in the lake, the causeway with bridges one after the other, and before us the great city of Mexico . . . Look, curious readers, isn't there much to think about in what I am writing? What men have ever in the whole world shown such boldness?"

Avid for fame, the great commanders were also touched in varying degrees by crusading zeal. Individual leaders differed widely in this regard, ranging from Francis Drake, whose piety never exceeded conventional English limits, to Queiros, who was a religious fanatic on the Iberian pattern. Certainly, like almost all men in that period, commanders took Christianity for granted. Most of them, however, would have been brought up on the most popular escape literature of the day, the chivalrous romances which portrayed Christian knights fighting pagans and grappling with the monsters and enchantments of strange climes. With this background, explorers may have seen themselves as popular heroes rather than as descendants of the medieval Crusaders.

The availability of ambitious captains and skilled crewmen, the pressure of material needs and the possession of an advanced technology, explain why the Europeans, of all the peoples then on earth, were able to launch the Age of Exploration.

But no great endeavor can be sustained without the fuel of ideology. Europe's ideology was compounded of various elements. Psychologically, Europeans as a whole were distinguished from other peoples at this time by an individualism that promoted action. In spite of the privileges exercised by kings, feudal lords, priests and guilds, the individual's freedom of action was less circumscribed than in caste-divided India, or in family-centered China, or under the priest-kings of Central and South America. Moreover, in spite of plagues and local famines, the standard of living in Europe was higher than elsewhere. Revolutions are the work not of the cowed and starving but of those who have enough to want more: Renaissance Europe, having recovered from the ravages of the terrible Black Death plague of the 14th Century, was sufficiently comfortably off to want to become rich.

Institutionally, Europe was a densely packed mosaic of thriving, thrusting, independent states, jealous of one another, determined not to be left behind in any race for power or wealth. Where Portugal led, Spain was bound to follow, France to envy, England to intervene.

In addition, the Europeans were Christians, and Christianity, notwithstanding its monasteries and mystics, was—of all the creeds existing in the world of Columbus' day—the one most suited to men of action. In Christianity, Europeans had a militant and expansionist religion that in practice allowed as much scope for profit as for prophets.

Christianity's nearest rival was Islam, whose warriors surged westward in triumph, taking Constantinople in 1453, threatening to conquer all Europe. Mohammedans were sustained in their military ardor by the belief that death in a battle against infidels meant an eternity of bliss in a heavenly harem. Christian morality, by contrast, emphasized the good life more than the worthy death. Moreover, after conquest, Islam was tolerant of other faiths to an extent far beyond anything Christianity could feel during the Renaissance or, indeed, for long after. Christians believed that the way they thought and lived was superior in every way to the customs of other peoples. The canny merchants and acquisitive kings who planned the explorations utilized this sense of superiority to justify their actions. When the rulers of Portugal explored Africa and broke into the Indian Ocean, they did so with a Bible in one hand and a sack for gold in the other.

Competitive and covetous nations, suitable ships,

a dynamic Christian outlook—it is curious that none of these factors arose directly from the values normally associated with the Renaissance as a great period of cultural brilliance. Why was it that while the artistic and intellectual Renaissance is primarily associated with Italy until the middle of the 16th Century, the chief exploring powers during that time were Portugal and Spain, countries on the very fringe of the esthetic revival?

Many of the greatest triumphs of the Age of Exploration did in fact owe their success to Italian scholars and seamen—themselves affected by the revival of learning in Italy. To understand how this came about, it is helpful to review the events of this period in Italy and the rest of Europe.

The renewed cultural activity in Italy early in the 14th Century was, initially, a straightforward response to a practical need. The vitality of Italy's political and economic life, and the high proportion of city dwellers in the small medieval states, created a stronger demand for secular education—especially legal education—than in the other countries of Europe. But as legal training increasingly involved the study of ancient Roman law, more attention came to be paid to other branches of Roman learning and literature.

By the middle of the 14th Century the interest in ancient precedent had produced a general ferment of ideas which influenced poetry and philosophy, architecture and medicine—fields far removed from business and government, whose demands had first spurred the classical revival. And this process went forward steadily, reaching its height with the writings of Machiavelli and the sculpture of Michelangelo in the 16th Century.

Even though Italy was plagued by wars, its decentralized structure enabled it to escape the paralysis that conflict brought to the nation-states of Europe. When one Italian region was struck by battles, others continued to flourish, and because

Italians mainly used hired mercenaries to fight their wars, life in the cities could still function more or less as in time of peace.

In the rest of western Europe, wars put savage brakes on the movement toward cultural rebirth by cutting back patronage of the arts and the free interchange of scholarly ideas. Nevertheless, in practical matters Italy's neighbors did not lag far behind. In England, France, Portugal, Spain and the German states, trade was becoming more complex, government finance more rational.

In two eminently practical fields, cartography and navigation, Portugal and Spain achieved remarkable competence early in the Renaissance. These studies, so vitally important to explorers, did not depend on Italian classical scholarship, but drew instead on sources readily available on the Iberian peninsula—knowledge gained by experienced seamen, and geographical principles worked out by Arab mathematicians and cosmographers, who taught Spaniards and Portuguese the lessons learned in the great Moslem trade area that included the Levant, India and North Africa.

Thus prepared, it is not surprising that Portugal, which started exploring the West African coast early in the 15th Century, and Spain, which began to compete with her there around the middle of the century, were the first European countries to embark on a policy of discovery. Their shipping was a principal beneficiary of the fruitful interbreeding of Mediterranean and Atlantic types. Both countries were perfectly situated to take advantage of the steady winds that in spring and early summer took ships southwestward into the Atlantic and then shifted to bring them back again in the autumn. And the crusading spirit lasted longer in these countries than elsewhere in Europe: Spain did not oust the last Moslems until 1492.

If Spain and Portugal were the capable hands and feet of the exploration movement, Renaissance

A PERSIAN PERSEUS, *dotted with stars after the constellation of the ancient Greek holds Medusa's head in this drawing by the Arab cosmographer al-Sufi. Workin from Ptolemy's "Almagest," a Greek astronomical treatise long unknown to th West, Arab astronomers compiled atlases locating and naming hundreds of star their knowledge proved invaluable to early Spanish and Portuguese navigator*

Italy was its subtle brain. None of the small states of Italy was rich enough to send out a steady flow of expeditions, let alone sponsor colonization. Italian merchants concentrated on maintaining existing markets rather than discovering new and distant ones. It was in the sciences essential to exploration —mathematics, astronomy and geographical theory —that Italy pioneered, and here her new knowledge and her well-educated mariners would play a large part in the voyages of other nations.

Early in the Age of Exploration, when Portugal and Spain were the only active exploring nations, these two Iberian powers tried to keep their discoveries secret. But foreign merchants in Lisbon and Seville saw returning vessels unload the cargoes of spices, ivory, slaves and dyes; listened to seamen's gossip; bribed pilots and copied maps. All the information they gathered was sent home. Governments were fired by the thought of new riches and power, individuals saw a fresh path to wealth and adventure. First England, then France, then, toward the end of the 16th Century, the Netherlands entered the lists until exploration became a European movement.

Outsailing, outshooting and outwitting peoples who had no wish to be explored, let alone exploited, the Europeans thrust their way across the world, nowhere encountering either equal technological ability or an ideology that would support an effective resistance. For two centuries and more, European expeditions, with their few seamen, would enter unfamiliar waters all over the globe, take notes, snatch a few natives as hostages or interpreters and leave for home. They were followed by larger ships with merchandise, sometimes with soldiers and settlers.

Always the Europeans were recognized, either at once or after a short time, as enemies and exploiters. But almost always they were able to gain a foothold and dominate local shipping. Technology accounts for part of these extraordinary successes, but by no means all; the balance must be accounted for not in terms of gun against spear, but of will against will, temperament against temperament.

The less-advanced tribes like the Arawaks of the West Indies and the Tupinamba of Brazil offered the least resistance to European domination. The Iroquoian Indians, who lived in North America between the Carolinas and the Great Lakes, were primarily hunters, with a higher degree of political organization that enabled them to put up a fierce resistance. But their thinking handicapped them in coming to terms with the invaders. For these tribes animals, plants, stones, weapons were all connected with the world of spirits. Their perception was based on an acceptance of a world filled with magical objects. Unlike the Arawaks, they could not be exterminated, but they could be pushed back from areas which Europeans wished to occupy.

Much further advanced were the Maya of Yucatán and Guatemala, who had a stable agriculture, cities and a loosely federated political organization. They were more literate, used numbers—including the sophisticated concept of zero—and had a systematized hierarchy of gods. It was fortunate for the Spanish conquistadors that Maya weapons were more primitive than their thought processes, and that they had been weakened by civil wars before the Europeans arrived.

It is one of the somber ironies of history that the most advanced civilizations of the Americas, those of the Aztecs of central Mexico and the Inca of Peru, were more vulnerable to the Spaniards than most of the primitive ones. Against complete savages like the Chichimecs, the Spaniards could never win a battle that assured them of freedom from further warfare. But once the Aztecs and Inca had been defeated by Spanish arms, their intricate administrative systems could be taken over entirely. The people, used to order and obedience, served their new masters without question. Again, it was fortunate for the Spaniards that these nations, whose arts and engineering feats still astonish us, knew nothing of gunpowder, and were gravely weakened by political jealousies. Even here victory was partly due to the undeflectable will to win of the Spaniards, which pierced the fatalism basic to their opponents' characters as surely as European bullets pierced their flimsy shields.

In the Far East, Europeans of the 15th Century came face to face with the China of the Ming Dynasty. This was an empire whose intellectual and artistic achievements were more refined than those of Europe, so that the belief of the Chinese that their civilization was superior to all others rested on something more than blind arrogance. But partly for religious reasons, partly because of the inertia that beset a vast, intricate and corrupt bureaucracy, the Chinese displayed an almost senile complacence. The brashness of the Europeans, their eagerness for new things and their loud confidence appalled the Chinese. For their part Europeans were bewildered by China's decision to turn its back on the world and withdraw inside its own borders.

Matteo Ricci, an Italian Jesuit who went to China in 1582, and lived there until his death 28 years later, explained that the Chinese had no notion of the outside world, and that this ignorance was a cause, as well as a product of their dislike of outsiders. "When they saw on the map what an almost unlimited stretch of land and sea lay between Europe and the Kingdom of China, that realization seemed to diminish the fear our presence had occasioned." And while the intellectual life of Europe was becoming increasingly scientific, in China, "the study of mathematics and that of medicine," wrote Ricci, "are held in low esteem." Although they were baffled by the immense gulf of cultural differences that separated them from the Chinese, Renaissance explorers had sought Cathay far too long to accept the closed door as final. Naked aggression against so huge a country was beyond the explorers' powers, but they insisted on and finally secured trading privileges at the port of Canton.

In Japan the Europeans encountered another culture of exceptional brilliance. Along with a remarkable school of painting, Japan had an architecture that provided more harmoniously rational living spaces than Europe would build until the 20th Century. At the turn of the 16th Century, Japan was emerging from almost three centuries of near anarchy. At this juncture, the country could have chosen to look out into the world—as it did in so dramatic a fashion in the 19th Century. Instead the decision was taken to imitate China. In 1635, the government forbade any Japanese to leave the country—or to return to it from any contaminating residence abroad—on pain of death.

Alone of civilized peoples, then, Europeans of the Renaissance had the technical and psychological equipment and the economic background to carry out a sustained program of exploration. And wherever the explorers went they found peoples either too primitive or too ill armed, too confused by local rivalries or too indifferent to oppose them.

During the Age of Exploration, what Europeans decided to do, they could do. As they pushed, observed and swaggered about the globe, they had the strange immunity we might grant to a race of active and intelligent Martians: only the forces of nature could stop them. The explorers were not in the mainstream of Renaissance culture, but they possessed an essential component of Renaissance man. In no sphere can the individualism of the Renaissance be studied as meaningfully as in their story—a story of men facing the unknown for months, sometimes years at a time, trusting a little to theory and the support of experts and governments at home, but mostly to their own skill and courage and to their ability to improvise.

A TROPIC SUN *burns across the water, turning it into what Christopher Columbus called "this bloody ocean, seething like a pot on a hot fire."*

THE FEARSOME SEA

The open ocean was to 15th Century seamen what space is to present-day astronauts—except that the sailor knew less about where he was going and had fewer hopes of returning. He was afraid to sail the Atlantic coast of Africa beyond Morocco, for there he would enter the "green sea of darkness," an unnavigable swamp full of monsters that had been reported by Arab geographers. If he headed out across the Atlantic, he might drift close to the equator, where men turned permanently black and no life could be sustained. If he went north he would find himself in a frozen waste where Judas lurked near the mouths of hell. Worst of all, in any direction he would be far from land and a prey to all the elements. As Columbus' son Ferdinand wrote, the crew dreaded "the fire in lightning flashes, the air for its fury, the water for the waves, and the earth for the reefs and rocks."

Once a ship had entered the uncharted wastes of the ocean, it was subjected to every extreme whim of the weather. Maps of the period mistakenly showed a string of islands stretching all the way across the Atlantic, but sailors could not find them when beset by storms or when held immobile in the deadly calm equatorial zone called the doldrums.

divers great Stormes, terrible Lightnings, and much Thunder"

SIR FRANCIS DRAKE, 1577

Magellan's men were stricken with scurvy, a vitamin deficiency disease, but they crossed nearly 12,000 miles of the Pacific without sighting a single island where they could get fresh fruit and vegetables.

In violent gales sailors could only pray to God and hope for a miracle. Englishmen would sing "Helpe Lord for good and godly men"; Italians looked for "St. Elmo's fire"—a glow of static electricity on the mast and yards that was considered a portent of fair weather to come; Christopher Columbus read the Bible aloud. According to his journal, both the waves and the men were calmed when he recited the words Christ spoke to his disciples during a storm: "Fear not, it is I."

23

"If I had not succeeded in throwing a grapnel on to a large mass of ice, by which I could turn the ship...both the ship and we would have been lost that day"

CAPTAIN JENS MUNCK, 1619

After southern routes to the Orient had been discovered, explorers looked unsuccessfully for a northern passage around Canada or Siberia. Even though captains ordered logs, ropes and bedding to be tied over the gunwales, icebergs often bore through the padding and crushed the ships. Sailors sometimes wielded pikes for days, fending off ice floes. Some bergs, according to Danish explorer Jens Munck, "stood firm on the sea bottom in more than 40 fathoms [240 feet]" while rising "quite twenty fathoms above the water." Munck's expedition of 1619 set out with a crew of 64 men. Three survived.

"Through the darknesse and obscuritie of the foggie mist,
we were almost run on rocks and Islands before we saw them:
But God provided for us, opening the fogges that we might see"

Even after the hazards of the open sea had been safely eluded, reefs often barred the way to land, and thick fogs obscured rocky shores. Navigators had no sure way of ascertaining their longitude or speed, and in heavy weather they might well founder on dangerous shoals. Certain points along the new routes to the Orient were particularly difficult to negotiate. The west coast of Australia became the graveyard of Dutch seamen bound for Java, as the coast of Natal was for Portuguese sailors heading home from India. The unwieldy commercial vessels of the Spanish fleet met destruction year after year in the Atlantic; in 1590 fifteen ships were driven ashore by a storm in Mexico and in the following year, 16 were wrecked in the Azores. Cape Horn at the tip of South America and the Cape of Good Hope in Africa were so perilous that they long retarded trade with Asia.

Fog baffled the early Atlantic seamen who were used to sailing the Mediterranean, where fog is rare. It also made navigating by the sun and stars impossible. Martin Frobisher, who was heading for Lumley's Inlet in Canada, got lost in thick weather, miscalculated his latitude and ended up far off course near Hudson Bay. Fog was doubly fearsome because it was generally regarded as infectious; Shakespeare voiced a popular notion when he called fog a "foul contagious darkness in the air."

> *"Four boatswain-birds came
> to the ship, a great sign
> of land; so many birds of one
> kind together is a sign they
> are not strays or lost"*
>
> COLUMBUS LOG—
> BARTOLOME DE LAS CASAS, 1492

The sea bore the first tantalizing signs of land—a plant, a bit of bark, a branch. Then at last came the shout from the forecastle, proclaiming to the fleet that ahead lay a new-found territory.

On Columbus' first voyage he was repeatedly misled by false promises of land. In his journal he recorded that he had spied terns and boatswain-birds, which he then confidently—and incorrectly—stated "never depart from land more than twenty-five leagues." Even a whale made him hopeful, since he imagined they hugged the shore. The gulfweed that floats on the Sargasso Sea well east of the Bahamas he claimed came from some nearby islands. He even became convinced the sea water was becoming less salty.

Every sailor strained to be the first to sight the Indies and to win the prize—an annual stipend of $700. Pedro Yzquierdo claimed to be the first, but Columbus insisted that he himself was the winner. Columbus got the prize and Pedro went off to Africa in a rage and became a Moslem.

2

PRINCE HENRY'S CAPTAINS

For Europeans of medieval times, the world consisted of four continents—Europe, Africa, Asia and, vaguely apprehended, the vast *Terra Incognita* that was believed to be situated somewhere in the Southern Hemisphere. On contemporary maps, these land masses crammed the earth's surface and crowded out the oceans: the Atlantic was reduced to a narrow waterway, there was no Pacific, and Terra Incognita squeezed the Indian Ocean into an inland sea.

This geographical confusion was the product not only of the map makers' understandable ignorance, but of religious beliefs which exaggerated the cartographers' errors. By Christian tradition, Jerusalem was located at the center of the world; medieval map makers, therefore, piously drew the world as a wheel, with the Holy City at the hub of the three known continents, whose actual shapes and locations were hopelessly distorted as a consequence.

This picture of the world stood in sharp contradiction to that drawn by geographers of classical antiquity. Greeks and Romans had made far more accurate maps of the world, but most of these had been lost in the confusion of the Dark Ages. Among the surviving works to which Renaissance scholars had access was the *Geographia* of Ptolemy, an astronomer and geographer who had lived in Hellenized Egypt in the Second Century A.D. Although by the mid-15th Century cartographers were preparing maps that reflected Ptolemaic ideas, many people nevertheless continued to favor the Jerusalem-centered maps over maps based on classical tradition. They stubbornly insisted on having maps that showed their spiritual home more prominently than their actual one.

Although the medieval Europeans' knowledge of Asia and Africa was vague, they were fascinated by those continents. The Bible had made Asia, home of the three Magi, and Africa, legendary source of King Solomon's wealth, part of the background of every Christian. In addition, Europeans were heirs to the stories handed down about these regions since classical times. For Europeans of the 15th Century, these tales, further elaborated by medieval storytellers like Sir John Mandeville, made Asia and Africa the Lands of Marvels.

Somewhere in Africa, for instance, there was,

A STYLIZED VIEW OF MACAO, *a Portuguese colony on the China coast, was engraved about 1598 by the Flemish artist Theodor de Bry. Established in 1557, Macao was the main port of foreign trade with China for 300 years.*

according to popular belief, a river of gold that emptied into a seething tropical sea no man could reach and still live. Somewhere—in Africa? in Asia? both were equally lands of fantasy—was a land studded with treasures that were guarded by dragons and hovered over by legless birds who spent their whole lives in the air. Somewhere there were sheep as great as oxen; giants who could wade into the ocean and seize a ship in the grip of one hand; women whose eyes, made of precious stones, could slay an intruder with a single glance; and men with feet so big that, held aloft, they served as parasols. There were Christian marvels, too. From the 12th Century on there flourished the legend of Prester John, a Christian ruler of fabulous wealth and power whose dwelling place was set first in Asia, then somewhere in Africa. Well into the 16th Century the hope persisted that if only a European power could get in touch with him Africa might somehow be converted.

All these legends flourished because they could not be checked by observation. Europeans were almost totally ignorant about Asia and Africa. A few traders had reached India, but all other attempts by Europeans to penetrate Asia farther than Syria and Palestine had been blocked first by Persian, later by Moslem rulers. It was not until about 1250 that the colossal Mongol Empire, which stretched from China to south Russia, allowed Christians free passage through all its territories. Among the many travelers who took advantage of this breach in the Asian curtain was Marco Polo, a Venetian merchant whose remarkably accurate and detailed account of his journeys and his stay at the court of Kublai Khan during the latter part of the 13th Century became one of the most popular of medieval travel books. In the middle of the 14th Century, however, Christian travel ended as the Ottoman Turks closed the curtain again. Asian legend, now mixed even more confusingly with the facts re-

ported by Marco Polo, resumed its hold on Europe.

Africa was cloaked in even greater mystery than Asia, for in spite of a trade in slaves and gold from the North African ports, European merchants and travelers had never been allowed into the interior. By the beginning of the 15th Century, however, many Europeans were no longer willing to accept permanent exclusion from the fabled lands to the east and south. Recovery from the ravages of the Black Death and improvements in economic techniques tended to make Europe look outward in search of new sources of trade. Moreover, Renaissance businessmen urgently needed an increased supply of precious metals to lubricate the machinery of international commerce. There were other motives for exploration, among them the need to extend fishing grounds and, not least, the impulse to convert the heathen to Christianity. So the stage was set for a remarkable series of Portuguese expeditions down the African coast, sponsored by a most remarkable man, Prince Henry the Navigator, third son of King John I.

Tall and muscular, with blond hair inherited from his English mother, the 21-year-old Henry had fought with distinction during the Portuguese capture of Ceuta, on the northern Moroccan coast, in 1415. From traders at Ceuta, he had learned much about the gold routes across the Sahara leading up through Morocco, and was tempted to push south. He soon saw that to conquer Morocco, with its mountains and deserts, was beyond the power of a small country. But Portugal had the seafaring ability and was geographically well poised to intercept the traffic at its source, which was believed to be near the Gulf of Guinea. He set himself, then, two goals: to trace the source of the trade in gold, ivory, slaves and pepper, and to get in touch with Prester John, with whom he hoped to plan a crusade that would clear the Moslems from North Africa and the Holy Land once and for all. To achieve

these ends, Henry established at Sagres, on the Portuguese coast, a community of scholars dedicated to geographical studies. The knowledge they accumulated was to be transmitted to the captains of his expeditions.

The exploration of the west coast of Africa would seem to present no serious physical difficulties to seamen used to the stormy waters that bordered Portugal. But there were great psychological hazards to be overcome. It was widely believed that life was insupportable near the equator. Cape Nun, on the northwestern coast of Africa in latitude 29° north, was so named because of the legend that none of the seamen who ventured past it returned: beyond Cape Nun, it was rumored, the boiling sea destroyed all who were not already burned black by the vertical sun. Farther yet lay the Antipodes, where, according to many Churchmen, only monsters could live. For, since all men were descended from Adam, and no man could pass the tropics, what but monsters could survive in Terra Incognita? As a final deterrent, many men were convinced that Africa joined Terra Incognita and could not be circumnavigated anyhow.

An early stage in Henry's venture had been

the securing of bases on the island groups off the African coast, the Madeiras, the Canaries and the Azores. These provided the Portuguese both with a series of supply stations (for they are more suited to Europeans' health and diet than the African mainland) and with a security net to catch vessels blown off course on the voyage home.

The obstacles to the exploration of the African coast, real and imaginary, gradually evaporated as seamen cautiously coasted south, approaching the unknown cape by cape from the security of the known. Cape Bojador, some 350 miles beyond Cape Nun, was passed in 1434. In 1441 an expedition returned from the Rio de Ouro region with a cargo of slaves, commencing the inhuman trade with Africa whose results still haunt us. By 1445 two more important headlands had been passed: Cape Blanco, named from the dazzling whiteness of its sands, and Cape Verde (site of present-day Dakar), so called for the profusion of evergreens that covered it. In that year, Dinis Dias, cruising off Cape Verde, saw that the coast began to trend toward the east. Had Africa been rounded?

It had not, of course; but, full of hope, and encouraged by the increasingly profitable European market for African slaves, expedition after expedition nudged the frontier of European knowledge farther south. Some of these parties were sponsored by the Crown, some were privately financed; some were bent on discovery, others were content to ship slaves from coasts already explored. Few details of these voyages are known because of the secrecy with which the Portuguese government surrounded them. Occasionally there is a glimpse of the explorers' characters, as when Alvise da Cadamosto proudly describes his eating elephant flesh on the Gambia River in 1456: "I had a portion cut off, which, roasted and broiled, I ate on board ship . . . to be able to say that I had eaten of the flesh of an animal which had never been previously eaten by any of my countrymen. The flesh, actually, is not very good, seeming tough and insipid to me."

Prince Henry died in 1460, and with him died much of the driving force that had inspired Portuguese explorers for more than 40 years. In the two decades that followed, exploration did not come to an absolute halt; for one thing, the equator was crossed in 1473 by Lopo Gonçalves without anyone bursting into flames or turning black. The crusading zeal persisted; captured natives, coached in the language and impressed with the wealth of Portugal, were released at intervals along the coast in the hope that they would make their way to Prester John. However, the search for Africa's gold had proved disappointing. Now the coveted prize was the spices of the Indies. But to get to India, Africa would first have to be rounded, and this goal continued to recede into the distance as navigators found the African coast stretching ever southward.

Portugal was no longer alone in its ambitions. As early as 1459, Spain began to put forth her claims to the few healthy, convenient and protected ports that were scattered along the enormous African coast. The swamps, deserts or fierce currents that separated these harbors presented forbidding obstacles to successful settlement elsewhere.

The Portuguese, having gotten there first, were determined to keep Africa to themselves, and they turned to the Pope for assistance. For centuries the Holy See had acted as arbitrator of disputes among all Christian nations. While this role was still taken for granted, papal decisions were beginning to lose some of the weight they had formerly possessed. Nevertheless, from 1455 on, the Portuguese secured from the Pope a series of pronouncements granting them all the lands and islands south of Cape Bojador. In about 1478 Ferdinand and Isabella, monarchs of Aragon and Castile, had tacitly acknowledged Portugal's exclusive rights in Africa by asking the Pope for formal permission to trade with Guinea. Although this request was refused, Spanish interlopers continued to visit the Gulf of Guinea in search of slaves.

The Portuguese must have known about the many clandestine expeditions from Castile to West Africa, for cargoes of Negro slaves had become a familiar quayside scene in Seville. Spanish activity —and that of the English, who in 1481 asked papal permission for African trading rights—acted as a spur to King John II, who came to the throne that same year. From then on, Portuguese explorers were once more prodded to new accomplishments as they had not been since Prince Henry's time. One of the new King's earliest acts was to dispatch Diogo Cão on the first of a series of Portuguese expeditions to find a sea route around Africa to India.

The voyages of Cão had one feature that reflects Portugal's determination to assert its claims to the African coast. He was supplied with *padrões*, stone pillars, inscribed in Latin, Portuguese and Arabic, which he was to erect on conspicuous landmarks as he discovered them. He set one up at the mouth of the Congo River, which he reached in 1483, and another at his southernmost landfall, Cape Cross, in 21° 50′ south of the equator.

Cāo opened up some 1,500 miles of coastline from Cape St. Catherine to Cape Cross, but the continent still ran southward, apparently endlessly. This did not deter John, and in 1487 the King sent out Bartolomeu Dias (no relation to Dinis Dias) with three ships to do still better; he was to try to circumnavigate Africa and, if possible, attempt to get in touch with Prester John.

The prospect was daunting. But by this time, the dreaded tropics had been crossed and recrossed, and it had been proved that the Europeans' armor and firearms enabled them to land and take on supplies wherever they wished, even if the natives were hostile. The Portuguese had gained so much respect that, according to a contemporary account, an African chief defeated a rival by ordering "his men, who were Negroes, to whiten their faces, legs and arms with clay . . . masquerading them in all other ways so that they might even more readily be taken for Christians." Confronted by this sight the enemy took to their heels "to the accompaniment of a great victory and much merriment."

Dias' voyage, like all the Portuguese expeditions, was veiled in secrecy. While few of the details of the journey are known, it certainly surpassed every previous venture in performance and in promise for the future. After Dias had reached the latitude of present-day Lüderitz in southwestern Africa, some 520 miles northwest of the Cape of Good Hope, he was swung away from the coast by violent storms. When the gales slackened and Dias found the shelter of land, he was in Mossel Bay, unaware that he had been blown clear around the Cape. He continued his voyage, going along a coast that trended gradually northeastward, as far as the Great Fish River near present-day Port Alfred.

By now he was convinced that he had passed the southernmost tip of Africa. But his crew had had enough. The old legends of unearthly perils had long been disproved, but seamen could still be seized by panic; Dias' men forced him to turn back —at the very gates of the Indian Ocean. Reluctantly he set a course for home, compensated in part on the return voyage by seeing the great promontory that he had circumnavigated. He called it the Cape of Storms, but King John, when he heard the news, looked to the future which Dias had made possible and renamed it the Cape of Good Hope.

In the same year that he sent Dias to find a sea route to India, King John dispatched two other emissaries on overland journeys, one to find a way to the riches of the East, the other to locate Prester John. Pero da Covilhā was instructed to go to India via Arabia and discover what he could about the routes used by the Moslem spice ships that crossed the Indian Ocean to Africa. The other explorer, Afonso de Paiva, was to penetrate Africa from the northeast, for the whereabouts of Prester John was becoming narrowed down to the region of Ethiopia. It is known that Covilhā spoke Arabic; Paiva probably did so also. The two men traveled together to Aden and then separated.

The silence that then descends on their movements is even more provoking than the mystery that shrouds the details of Dias' voyage. All that is known is that Covilhā found his way to Calicut, on the west coast of India (not to be confused with Calcutta, on the east coast). Here junks from China and the East Indies brought spices, porcelain, silks and gems. Together with the pepper and ginger of the Malabar Coast, these precious goods were then transferred into the holds of merchantmen for shipment to the Persian Gulf and East Africa. Covilhā was not the first European visitor; the craft that regularly sailed from Cairo down the Red Sea and along the wind route to western India had at various times carried Venetian, Genoese, French and Dutch traders. Following their route in reverse, Covilhā sailed back to the Persian Gulf and reached Sofala, just south of Beira. There, it is likely, he learned that the Indian Ocean joined the South Atlantic, thus making possible a sea passage from Europe to India.

In 1490 Covilhã arrived in Cairo to rendezvous with Paiva, only to find that his fellow traveler had died there. Waiting for Covilhã, however, were messengers with new instructions from the King: Covilhã was to report on his progress and then take over Paiva's mission as well as his own. He found his way to the Ethiopian court, but there was no sign of Prester John and the Ethiopian king refused to let him return home. In 1520, when another mission reached the court, it received a surprise welcome from an aging Covilhã, one of the most touching and remarkable victims of his country's urge to expand. For there is little doubt that his report concerning the Indian Ocean had reached Lisbon and helped to sustain John II, who died in 1495, and his successor King Manuel, in their drive to open the sea route to India.

The man chosen by Manuel to follow up Dias' lead was Vasco da Gama. Little is known about Da Gama. He was born in 1460, the son of a minor official, and he must have had a good record as a seaman to justify his appointment. Dias, hero of the hour, was called in to supervise the construction of three stout square-rigged vessels, the flagship *São Gabriel*, the *São Raphael*, and a storeship whose name has been lost; a fourth ship, the *Berrio*, was lateen-rigged. The choice of square rigging was Dias', made in the light of the buffeting his lateen-rigged caravels had taken in the South Atlantic. It was possibly on Dias' advice, too, that Da Gama adopted the revolutionary policy of swinging far west into the Atlantic from the vicinity of Sierra Leone, thus avoiding coastal squalls and currents, until he could pick up the westerlies that would bring him to the Cape of Good Hope.

On July 8, 1497, Da Gama left Lisbon harbor. Following the suggested sailing directions, he dis-

covered the wind route between Europe and the Cape that has been followed by windjammers ever since. After three months and a voyage of nearly 4,000 miles, Da Gama reached the African coast at St. Helena Bay, just north of Cape Town, and continued past Cape Agulhas to Mossel Bay. There he broke up the storeship and reprovisioned the other ships from it.

At Mossel Bay, Da Gama erected a *padrão* (which was promptly pulled down by the natives), and then continued eastward. The names he gave to coasts and rivers—Natal, named for Christmas, Christ's natal day; the River of Good Omens—reflected his optimism as the coast turned more northerly and the sea became warmer.

At last, after seeing nothing but thousands of miles of open sea and savage country, he sailed into the thriving port of Mozambique, where large merchantmen of unfamiliar shape were anchored in the roadstead, and Arabs and native traders haggled on the quays. Instead of encountering naked chiefs who chattered excitedly when thrown a handful of little bells, he was greeted by a sultan who treated the Portuguese trade goods with contempt and demanded scarlet cloth, which Da Gama did not have.

In spite of the shock of this sudden reacquaintance with sophistication, Da Gama retained his optimism. One of his sailors, who had picked up Arabic while a prisoner of the Moors, acted as translator and Da Gama learned that farther north there were great ports where spices, pearls and rubies were traded. According to a journal kept by one of his men, Da Gama was told "that Prester John resided not far from this place; that he held many cities along the coast. . . . The residence of Prester John was said to be far in the interior, and could be reached only on the back of camels." As information this could hardly have been more misleading, but as news it was welcome. So, after se-

D. VASCO DA GAMA. VI.

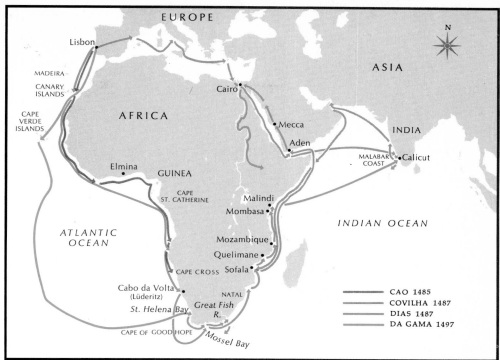

curing a local pilot, Da Gama pressed on due north.

The next leg of Da Gama's journey was filled with adventures. His pilot was not as skillful as he might have been, and Da Gama had him flogged for mistaking the Kerimba Islands for the mainland. Later the *São Raphael* ran aground on a shoal, but it was mid-tide and the vessel floated free when the tide rose. At Mombasa, a thriving Arab port in present-day Kenya, the Portuguese were the object of great suspicion and an attempt was made by the local inhabitants to capture the flagship. Now very suspicious, Da Gama had two captive Moors "questioned" (even the journal used quotation marks) "by dropping boiling oil upon their skin, so that they might confess any treachery intended against us." The information Da Gama secured from this interrogation made him decide it was safe to move up the coast to Malindi, where, to his great joy, the sultan welcomed the Portuguese.

Da Gama found a community of Hindus living in Malindi, and he was unshakably convinced that they were Christians—a sign that the elusive Prester John was not far away. But best of all, Da Gama managed to hire a new pilot, a Gujarati from western India, who not only offered to guide him across the Arabian Sea but turned out to be one of the most learned and experienced pilots of his age. With this able man aboard, Da Gama took his squadron east into the Indian Ocean; they were the first European ships to be seen there.

The port in west India where Da Gama at last dropped anchor was Calicut, already known from Covilhã's report of 1490 as one of the foremost trading cities of the Malabar Coast. To the Arabs and Persians who dominated the trade between Africa and India, the previous appearances of Europeans on the Malabar Coast had offered no threat. The visitors from the west were too few, and their individual efforts too uncoordinated to present a challenge to merchants and shippers who had dominated the profitable traffic for generations. However, the coming of Da Gama's little fleet was another matter entirely. For it was evident that a high degree of organization had been required to send Da Gama's expedition halfway around the world. And this meant that a European king was determined to become an important factor in the Indies trade. Put on warning, the Moslem traders reacted with considerable jealousy and resistance.

Da Gama's stay in Calicut was therefore unsatisfactory from a trading point of view. He found the greatest difficulty in disposing of his wares and buying others. There was also a plot against his life which was foiled through a warning given by a friendly Moor. To the ever-optimistic Portuguese this attempt at murder was especially shocking, for they were convinced, as they had been in Malindi, that the Indians themselves, as opposed to the Moslem merchants, were Christians. So certain were they of this that they persuaded themselves that a Hindu temple was a church and a statue of the goddess Devaki a madonna. "They threw holy water over us," the journal recounted, "and gave us some white earth, which the Christians of this country are in the habit of putting on their foreheads, breasts, around the neck, and on the forearms. . . . Many other saints were painted on the walls of the church, wearing crowns. They were painted variously, with teeth protruding an inch from the mouth, and four or five arms."

Finally, on August 29, 1498, Da Gama decided that little more could be accomplished and he set sail for Portugal. The stretch across the Indian Ocean took three months and so many men died of scurvy that Da Gama had to abandon and destroy the *São Raphael* near Mombasa because he no longer had enough seamen to work her. The rest of the voyage was without major incident. When Da Gama sailed into Lisbon harbor in September 1499, he had been away more than two years and had sailed 24,000 nautical miles. Of the 170 men who had left Lisbon, only 44 returned.

Europe responded to the news of Da Gama's success with combined rejoicing and alarm. King Manuel wrote jubilantly to Ferdinand and Isabella that "as the principal motive of this enterprise has been . . . the service of God our Lord, and our own advantage, it pleased Him in His mercy to speed them on their route." Not only was a new world opened to missionary endeavor but "henceforth," Manuel gloated, "all Christendom, in this part of Europe, shall be able . . . to provide itself with these spices and precious stones."

But merchants and traders with a stake in the long-established routes to the spice markets of the eastern Mediterranean were dismayed. The Portuguese, as always, imposed the tightest secrecy on the details of the route that Da Gama followed. All that the rest of Europe knew was that he had reached India. Frantic efforts were made, particularly by Italians, to find out through spies and bribery the exact nature of Da Gama's voyage. An entirely new era of world trade was opening.

Another was closing—when Da Gama sailed from Malindi to India, the Renaissance exploration of the African coast was to all intents finished. In 1500 one of the ships from the next Portuguese expedition, driven off course, discovered Madagascar, and later in the century detailed surveys were made of the southeast African coast. But the explorations that followed Da Gama's trail-blazing journey, while necessary and useful, had none of the impact of his first venture into the Indian Ocean.

Da Gama's achievement in reaching India puts him in the first rank of explorers of all time. The distance he had to cover, the difficulty of making his landfall north of the Cape after the long sweep out into the Atlantic, the problems posed by the fierce currents running against him off Mozambique and elsewhere—these hazards required a courage and skill of seamanship that were equal to those possessed by his remarkable contemporary, Christopher Columbus. Like Columbus, Da Gama helped give Europeans an entirely new concept of the world in which they lived; man was no longer restricted to the three known continents and their neighboring waters. The whole world was open to him to explore and exploit.

AFFLUENT ARTISTS, *the officers of the artists' guild, painted by Jan de Bray, display the self-satisfaction typical of the Netherlands' Golden Age.*

THE PROSPEROUS TRADERS

While Spain and Portugal ranged the world in search of gold and converts, other countries sought out the new lands for trade. Of these, the small but vigorous Netherlands ultimately reaped Europe's greatest harvest of prosperity. By 1629, Dutch burghers, whose business sense led them to select tough captains for their well-armed ships, could claim to have "sailed all other nations off the seas . . . [and] drawn almost all trade from other lands." The Dutch became Europe's largest importers and distributors of spices, sugar, porcelain and decorative beads. They spent the enormous profits from this trade on middle-class pleasures, filling their houses with valuable furnishings, wearing beautiful fabrics, loading tables with lavish meals. When such spending could not absorb all the money that poured in, they turned to art, which they often commissioned to commemorate themselves or their possessions. At first only by-products of prosperity, many of these paintings became the enduring monuments of 17th Century Dutch achievement.

A WELL-LADEN FLEET

Salt water exercised the greatest single influence on Dutch life, providing both the means and the necessity for the country's booming trade. North Sea harbors, which had always given the Netherlands access to European markets, also opened

on the new world. Towering ships such as those in the fleet above, painted by H. C. Vroom as they returned home fully laden from Brazil, brought wealth to the entire country. The need of the Dutch to earn their bread on the water was, itself, determined by water: with two fifths of the Netherlands below sea level, and dunes, bogs and lakes limiting the use of available land, much of the population depended, directly or indirectly, upon the success of seafaring trade.

AN ABUNDANT TABLE *is heaped with turkey, which was first found in the Americas, as well as succulent fruit and lobster. Still-life painting such as this work by Abraham van Beyeren first flourished in the Netherlands.*

A RICH LIFE AT HOME

Trade from overseas spread riches throughout all Dutch society, and nowhere was this more evident than in the gusto the Dutch brought to eating, drinking and smoking. Food was available in vast quantities; wine and beer from France and Germany flowed endlessly, and tobacco—powdered as snuff or cut to smoke in long clay pipes—was the companion of every occasion. Even beggars had their snuffboxes, from which they often took a pinch before soliciting a coin. Pipe-making became a major industry, for at home a man might smoke four or five pipes one after the other. He could even listen to hymns honoring this "medicinal herb."

A MERRY FAMILY, *three high-spirited generations enjoy their own company, as well as good food and bagpipe music, in Jan Steen's painting. Women used foot warmers (lower left) because men usually got the seats nearest the fire.*

A HOUSEHOLD'S TREASURES

The good burgher of the Netherlands cherished a genuine love for his house. He spent virtually all his time away from work within its shelter, and he felt justified in lavishing great amounts of money on its furnishings. Such invested wealth showed up in cabinets, tables, chairs and luxurious bric-a-brac as well as crockery and kettles, which the industrious housewife maintained with almost fanatical tidiness. Food was prepared in a small recessed pantry to preserve the kitchen's orderliness. Children who might disarrange things were generally banished from the house, except for meals and at bedtime. Dutch youngsters, rich and poor, had to play all day in the sunshine and fresh air.

SCRUPULOUS HOUSEWIFE *(below) counts her [lin]en with the help of a servant. Linen cup[bo]ards, the pride of every house, might [ho]ld as many as 24 dozen shirts and 40 doz[en] tablecloths and napkins. The little girl is [pl]aying "kolf," an ancestor of today's game.*

A PARROT FROM THE INDIES—*probably brought home on a Dutch sailor's shoulder—makes a proper companion for a lady wearing an elegant fur-trimmed crimson jacket in a portrait by Frans van Mieris.*

CHINESE MING BOWLS, *seen beside a Dutch-made pewter flagon, came from the Orient on Dutch ships carrying cargoes of spices and tea. Well-to-do Dutch homes were filled with such precious objects.*

FROM PROSPERITY
A WEALTH OF ART

Searching for a sensible way to spend their money, the Dutch discovered art both as a pleasure and as a business. The art dealer, who sold from a gallery such as the one shown here, also acted as an important intermediary between painters and their patrons. His trade was brisk. The demand for Dutch paintings extended to the court of Louis XIV of France and aristocratic collectors in Italy and England, but the major market was the Dutch middle class. The burghers often liked art not so much for esthetic reasons as because paintings could attest to their new riches. Above all, they wanted faithful renderings of the familiar aspects of their lives, and painters were happy to comply. Most Dutch artists were simply good craftsmen and they produced great quantities of meticulous interiors and seascapes, as well as group portraits of families, civic magistrates and merchants with their fleets. But others— such as Jan Vermeer, Frans Hals, Jan Steen and Rembrandt van Rijn—rode the tide of Dutch prosperity to produce deathless art.

A PRIDE IN TRADE

The Dutch Golden Age came about, in great part, because of the unique qualities of men such as the prosperous trader seen above, holding hands with his wife on a hill near the port of Batavia (now Jakarta, Indonesia). He permits a servant to

shield him against the sun with a parasol, but he stubbornly clings to the plain clothes of home. East India Company ships, to which he soberly points, brought merchants dividends as high as 50 per cent. The Dutch, having thus taken advantage of the expanded world, were well pleased with themselves. Even their contemporaries from other European countries "never tired of admiring the happiness of the subjects of the States of Holland and could not help envying their condition."

N

GREENLAND

ERIC THE RED
c. 980

ICELAND

NORWEGIANS
Late 9th Century

NORWAY

LEIF ERICSON c. 1000

NORTH
AMERICA

Westerlies

EUROPE

SPAIN

1493

Horse Latitudes

COLUMBUS 1492

*ATLANTIC
OCEAN*

AFRICA

Northeast Trades

SOUTH
AMERICA

WINDS FOR SEAFARING *favored the earliest explorers, as the map above shows. Ei-
by luck or by shrewd observation (historians disagree on the point), Columbus
ked the best routes out and back, as Leif Ericson probably did some 500 years earlier.*

searching for additional evidence to buttress his cause.

King John II of Portugal, after careful consideration, turned him down. When Spain's joint rulers, Ferdinand and Isabella, agreed, it was only after years of debate. While the experts at the Spanish court questioned the matter of his argument, the Queen was convinced by his manner, which gave the impression of utter certainty. Other factors influenced her decision, to be sure, one of them being the insistence of Luis de Santangel, keeper of the King's privy purse, who pricked her pride by offering to finance the expedition himself. Another important consideration was Spain's inability to gain any official part of the lucrative West African trade controlled by Portugal.

With royal backing, Columbus departed for Palos, a busy port in southwestern Spain, to obtain ships and crews. Two of the vessels, the *Niña* and the *Pinta*, were caravels about 70 feet long. The commander's flagship, the *Santa María*, was somewhat larger, but inferior in sailing qualities to the other vessels. Recruiting crews and fitting out the ships occupied Columbus for about 10 weeks. Then, on the morning of August 3, 1492, Columbus attended early mass and went aboard the *Santa María*. Shortly before sunrise, the ships weighed anchor and quietly drifted out of the harbor on the ebb tide, for there was no wind. Once in the open sea, they caught a breeze and Columbus set the course, south by west. His first destination was the Canary Islands, which were on the latitude Columbus intended to sail along and from which he knew the winds blew to the west at that time of year.

The winds out of the Canaries indeed proved favorable, and blew even more steadily than he could have hoped for. One day the ships covered 182 miles, averaging almost eight knots, extremely good speed for sailing ships of any era. Columbus' chief concern was the morale of his men. He was careful

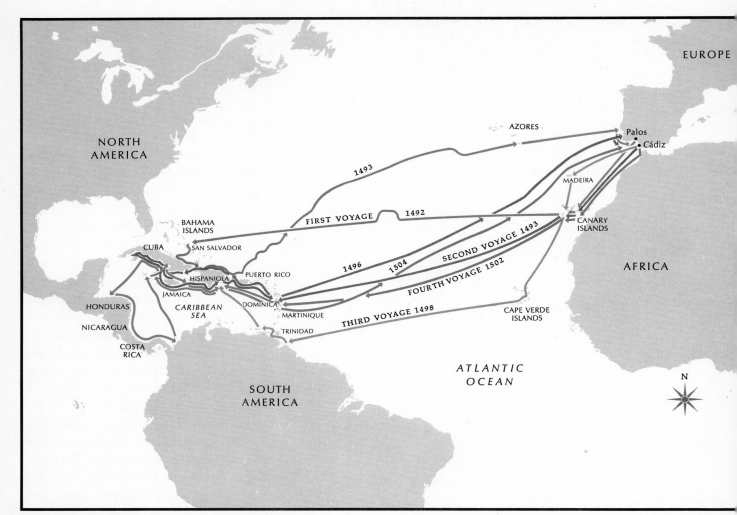

COLUMBUS' HISTORIC VOYAGES *are charted above. There are four outbound but only three homebound: for failing to keep order in Hispaniola, he was sent home from one trip as a prisoner.*

to make two reckonings of the distance covered: one which he kept to himself, and a deliberate underestimate which he announced to the crew. By minimizing the distance traveled, he hoped to guard against their panic at being so far into the unknown. Things went so well—no storms or long calms, no damage to the ships, plenty of food—that the voyagers' very good luck became a cause of anxiety. Once they had all been longer at sea than ever before in their experience, the men were seized by one fear after another. The weather was fine: would it ever rain—or would they all die of thirst? The winds were steady:

would they ever find winds to blow them home again—or did all the winds blow from the east in this unknown sea? After they struck the loose weed mat of the Sargasso Sea the sailors were haunted by the thought that the ships would get stuck and never get out. By October 10, nerves were at breaking point.

On the *Santa María*, after 30 days at sea, the crew demanded that Columbus turn back, and at last he promised to do so if they did not sight land within two or three days. It was enough. Two days later, at 2 a.m., October 12, the three ships were running easily before the trade winds under a moon just past the full, when the lookout on the forecastle of the *Pinta*, which was in the lead, cried out "Land! Land!" Columbus brought up the *Santa María*, confirmed it to be a true landfall and ordered the fleet to stand off at a safe distance from the surf until dawn. It was the little Bahama island of San Salvador, or Watling's Island. Later that day, Columbus and his men went ashore and became the first Europeans to set foot on the Caribbean islands.

They also had their first meeting with the inhabitants of San Salvador, gentle Arawak Taino Indians, who greeted the explorers with friendly courtesy and eagerly exchanged gifts with the crew. To Columbus, the tiny gold nose ornaments worn by the Indians offered incontrovertible evidence that he had reached the Indies. He noted in his journal: "I intend to go and see if I can find the Island of Japan."

So he set sail. When he discovered Cuba 15 days later he thought he had surely found Japan, Marco Polo's Cipangu, though, puzzlingly, there were no silk-clad sages or palaces tiled with solid gold. From the inlet now called Puerto Gibara, he dispatched into the interior as impressive an embassy as he could assemble from his ragged company. Luis de Torres, who led the group, was a converted Jew "who knew Hebrew and Aramaic and even some Arabic"—languages that might be useful at the Chinese court, to which he was to present his passport, gifts and letters of credence from Ferdinand and Isabella. Torres was accompanied by Rodrigo de Xeres, who had once called on an African king and thus qualified as an envoy to an exotic court, and by two Indians. The quest was disappointing, for of course Torres found nothing that faintly resembled an imperial city. But he and Xeres did observe Indians smoking cigars, making this the first European encounter with tobacco.

While the little procession was off on its mission,

Columbus took a steady star sight and worked out his latitude; then, by totaling the ships' daily runs since leaving the Canaries, he arrived at what he thought was his longitude. His conclusion was that he was not in Japan after all; by his estimate he had sailed too far from Europe for that. No, this was China. Or, as he decided a little later, he had discovered a group of islands, hitherto unknown, off the mainland of Cathay.

For three months following his first landfall on October 12, Columbus moved his little fleet through the uncharted and often dangerous waters around the Bahamas, Cuba and Hispaniola, from time to time capturing Indians to take back to Spain. On Hispaniola he was again elated by the sight of gold ornaments worn by villagers and by a hammered gold mask he received as a gift. Toward the end of this cruise he lost his flagship, the *Santa María*, when she went aground near Cap Haitien one dark night. But her timbers were salvaged to house the first European settlement in the New World, a fort which Columbus garrisoned with 40 crewmen.

Then he decided it was time to set a homeward course, to bring his sovereigns the great news that the Enterprise had been no mere vision, and that contact had been made with Cathay.

On the mistaken assumption that the way back to Spain lay northeast by east (a heading that would have brought him to the Arctic) Columbus set that course for his ships, and through this accident he stumbled on the secret of the fastest eastward passage: north to the latitude of Bermuda, where the prevailing winds blow from the west. But after a month of wonderful progress, Columbus ran into a fierce succession of storms, from which he emerged exhausted but safe off the island of Santa María in the Azores. The trip from there to the mainland was equally storm-wracked, and the weary mariners were glad to take shelter at last in Lisbon harbor on March 4.

During the fine sailing weather of the early part of the voyage from Hispaniola to the Azores, Columbus had found time to write a long letter to Ferdinand and Isabella, calculated to whet their appetites for a personal report from his own lips, and he now sent this letter ahead from Lisbon. He told of islands off the Cathayan coast, rich in spices and gold, and with timid and affectionate inhabitants who could without difficulty be converted to Christianity. Of the islands' beauty Columbus wrote with an eloquent love of nature rarely encountered in his day. Describing the mountains of Hispaniola he wrote: "All are most beautiful, of a thousand shapes, and all accessible, and filled with trees of a thousand kinds and tall, and they seem to touch the sky. . . . And there were singing the nightingale and other little birds of a thousand kinds in the month of November."

His enthusiasm for the beauty of the mountains, beaches, pastures and palms of the West Indies was justified, but his account of their riches, based on the discovery of a few personal ornaments of gold, was wildly exaggerated. This exaggeration was like the juggling of distance he had done for his crew: a lure to enable less idealistic men to attain the truth of his own vision. If he had not cheated over his distances, his men might have mutinied more than two days away from San Salvador. If he had not cheated over his gold, his patrons might not have sent him back again; primitive America would not have been wooed so soon or so passionately had her suitors not thought her to be sophisticated China.

Columbus returned to Palos, which he had last seen nearly eight months before, on March 15, 1493. One month later he was received in state by his delighted patrons, Ferdinand and Isabella, at their court in Barcelona. The monarchs had already indicated their pleasure by granting Columbus the titles promised for a successful voyage: he was henceforth to be addressed as "Don Cristóbal Colón . . . Admiral of the Ocean Sea, Viceroy and Governor of the Islands that he hath discovered in the Indies."

Now the King and Queen listened as the Admiral told how he had landed on some of the small islands off the Chinese coast and on one very large one which he called Hispaniola from its likeness to Spain, and how he had sailed some way along the coast of the mainland itself (actually part of the north coast of Cuba). The islanders he had brought back lent credence to his story precisely because of their primitive ways. For Marco Polo, the chief authority on eastern Asia, had not only described the fabulous wealth of China and Japan but had reported that between them were islands of savages who "have no king or chief, but live like beasts." Impressed by this evidence, Ferdinand and Isabella enthusiastically agreed to send Columbus back with a much more elaborate expedition, so that he could explore the mainland and find the court of the Great Khan himself.

To protect their expected access to the gold, the spices and the missionary opportunities of the East, the Spanish monarchs took a critical step: they applied to the pope for exclusive rights to trade and conquest across the Ocean Sea. Now the Church was to make a ruling of great historical significance. In a last gesture of global sovereignty, Rome would divide the world.

When the Spanish presented their petition they were following the precedent set by the Portuguese from 1455 on, when, to protect their discoveries along the African coast, they had obtained a series of papal bulls granting them a monopoly "in the Ocean Sea toward the regions lying southward and eastward." The Portuguese had interpreted this gigantic blank check as full title to the whole of the Atlantic south of the Canary Islands.

The assumption underlying the bulls was that

DIVIDING UP THE WORLD, *the pope in 1481 issued the bull "Aeterni regis," awarding all new lands south of the Canary Islands to Portugal, as shown. In 1493 he amended this to give all new lands east of 38° west longitude to Portugal and all those west of that meridian to Spain. Later, by treaty, the pope's line was moved to 46° 37' west—which eventually gave Portugal its toehold in Brazil.*

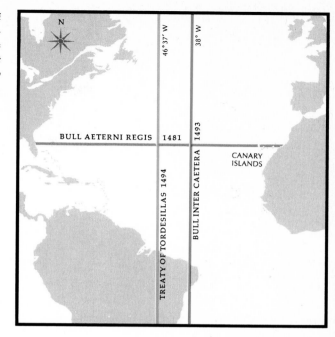

Portugal, as a crusading power, was doing the Church's work and was entitled to some secular perquisites. Spain's plea rested on the same grounds. Since Pope Alexander VI, head of the notorious Borgia clan, was himself a Spaniard who owed much of his successful career as a churchman to the favor of the Spanish Crown, he listened sympathetically to Spain's request for a free hand in the Ocean Sea— even though this would conflict with Portugal's prior claim to the South Atlantic. Ferdinand and Isabella asked for a vertical line that would cross Portugal's horizontal line 100 leagues (about 300 miles) west of the Azores, conceding to Portugal the areas east of the line. Setting the boundary at this point was Columbus' own idea: he had noticed changes in wind and the appearance of the sea, as well as rather unusual compass variation, which convinced him that here an invisible but real frontier divided the Ocean Sea.

Alexander did not hesitate. By the bull *Inter caetera* he granted to Spain everything she had demanded. The King of Portugal immediately objected, demanding that his horizontal line should be respected. After negotiation between the two powers a compromise was reached in June 1494 by the Treaty of Tordesillas. Under its terms, later endorsed by the Holy See, Spain's vertical line was shifted 270 leagues farther westward, to longitude 46° 37'. Among other things, this shot in the dark presented Portugal with Brazil, which wound up eastward of the new line.

If the Church had possessed any effective sanctions, the history of exploration would henceforth have concerned only Spain and Portugal. As it was, the Treaty of Tordesillas did have some influence in moderating the hot competition between these two countries. Some 25 years later, when Ferdinand Magellan, a Portuguese sailor in the service of Spain, set off to search for a passage to Cathay round the southern tip of South America, he was warned not to invade "the demarcation and limits of the most serene King of Portugal." But when voyage after voyage showed how great were the prizes to be won, and as other countries came to join in the race to secure them, neither the political nor the ecclesiastical sanctions of Tordesillas and *Inter caetera* had any power to stop them. Francis I, King of France, sarcastically remarked: "I should very much like to see the passage in Adam's will that divides the New World between my brothers, the Emperor Charles V [of Spain] and the King of Portugal." And by the middle of the 16th Century, when England was taking an increasing interest in discovery, Elizabeth's minister William Cecil sharply warned the Spanish ambassador that "the Pope had no right to partition the world and to give and take kingdoms to whomever he pleased."

In 1493, however, Spanish property rights seemed foolproof and Columbus was at the highest point in his career. The pattern of his life was set: For the next 10 years he would journey between Spain and his newly discovered lands, always convinced that he was on the verge of the long-awaited meeting with the rulers of Cathay.

In September 1493, with the Spanish claim fairly staked, Columbus set off again to see what it consisted of. After 21 days of beautiful sailing weather he was back in the Antilles. This time his landfall was the most northern of the Windward Islands, to which he gave the name Dominica, from the Italian word for Sunday, the day on which he sighted it. Thence he sailed the glamorous arc of the Leeward Islands, which curve northwest and west to Puerto Rico, naming them as they came in sight: Santa María de Guadalupe, Santa María de Monserrate (Montserrat), Santa Cruz (now called St. Croix) and many more—palm-fringed, their beaches blinding white, but with no Cathayan temple bells audible above the rhythmic sighing of the surf. Columbus moved quickly on to Hispaniola to inspect the tiny colony he had left behind at Navidad near Cap Haitien. He found that every man had been massacred by the natives—the first evidence that European settlers would have to battle to maintain their claims in this land across the sea.

Having established another settlement in Hispaniola, he then left in the *Niña* with two other ships on a continuation of what has been termed "the first West Indies cruise." The account of Columbus' physician, Dr. Chanca, conveys the atmosphere of a vacation trip. The weather was generally fair, the islands beautiful. The sailors saw their first hammock, ate their first yams. Everything was new, and much was wonderful. Dr. Chanca wrote with amazement about "trees bearing wool, of a sufficiently fine quality (according to the opinion of those who are acquainted with the art) to be woven into good cloth. . . . There are also cotton trees as large as peach trees, which produce cotton in the greatest abundance. We found trees producing wax as good both in color and smell as bees-wax and equally useful for burning, indeed there is no great difference between them." On the other hand, "there were wild fruits of various kinds, some of which our men, not very prudently, tasted; and upon only touching them with their tongues, their countenances became inflamed, and such great heat and

pain followed, that they seemed to be mad." The "wool trees" were actually the wild cotton bushes known today as Sea Island cotton; the cotton trees were the huge tropical trees whose fibers are now called kapok; the wax trees were one of several wax-producing palms; the stinging fruit was that of the manzanillo, or manchineel, tree, and its deadly poison was used by Carib Indians to tip their arrows.

There were simple local inhabitants whose customs startled the Europeans. For ceremonial occasions, in lieu of clothes, "both men and women paint themselves, some black, others white and various colors . . . they shave some parts of their heads, and in others wear long tufts of matted hair, which have an indescribably ridiculous appearance." Some of the islanders were cannibals, and Dr. Chanca saw human bones in their huts and "the neck of a man, undergoing the process of cooking."

While the doctor took his tourist notes, Columbus was still pressing his search for Cathay. This time he tried the south coast of Cuba, working his vessels westward along it—with a side trip in which he discovered Jamaica—until he came to Bahía Cortés, where the land begins to curve to the southwest.

At this point he stopped. His ships were leaking, his men were agitated by the old question: would they be able to get back? He was sure that he had reached the base of the Malay Peninsula. His own business lay farther north, in China, and he was convinced that the Great Khan could be found on another voyage.

The return trip, in the spring of 1496, was slow and arduous. In July, Columbus once more was received by Ferdinand and Isabella, to whom he gave the news that Cathay was within their grasp. Once more he extrapolated from a golden chain to a river of gold; once more he emphasized how easy it would be to make the savages—whom Dr. Chanca had seen eating spiders and worms—into pious and noble Christians.

In the course of his third and fourth voyages across the Atlantic, Columbus continued to make new discoveries. In May 1498 he left Spain for his third westward crossing, sailing much farther south than previously before heading west. He wanted to determine whether there was any basis in fact for the King of Portugal's conviction that there were continental lands somewhere out in the ocean, south and east of the Spanish discoveries. If such lands existed, it was important for Spanish explorers to reach them first and publish a Spanish estimate of their location. No one could then calculate longitude accurately, and if the new lands could be placed within the Spanish sphere, the claim would be difficult to disprove later on.

Columbus' landfall on his third voyage was Trinidad, another addition to his list of discoveries. A few days later, his crew landed on a beach near the delta of the Orinoco. At first he still insisted that he was among islands. Then, as he continued to investigate the Gulf of Paria, and felt the full push of the Orinoco's outlet against his ships, he changed his mind. No island could father a river with waters so vast. "I believe," he wrote, "that this is a very great continent, which until today has been unknown."

Then, denying his logical approach, he decided that this was not an entirely new continental mass he had reached but rather the threshold of the Earthly Paradise—the blessed domain whose whereabouts had been so earnestly debated by medieval geographers. Much as he longed to enter this enchanted realm, his sailors were grumbling and the supplies for the colony in Hispaniola were spoiling. So he turned north, leaving the further exploration of South America to other men.

One last voyage, his fourth, lay ahead for Columbus. He had already discovered the West Indies and the northern coast of South America—the Spanish Main. In the summer of 1502, he discovered Central America, touching first at Honduras, which he assumed was part of the Malay Peninsula. By this time Vasco da Gama had rounded Africa and reached India, putting Portugal far ahead on the road to Marco Polo's islands of spices and gold. So it was urgent that Columbus push south to find the strait that would give Spain equal access to those fabulous isles. Fighting adverse winds, the Admiral steered his fleet past Nicaragua and Costa Rica. In Panama he established a short-lived settlement at Belén. Then he continued on along the coast, but when he found the land trending southeasterly he stopped. The "Malay Peninsula" was larger than he had believed possible. This was the last of his discoveries.

He was back in Spain in 1504, and died two years later, 55 years old, utterly worn out, disgraced through the envy of rivals and by his inefficient record as a colonizer in Hispaniola. As an administrator he was fallible. But as a seaman, a leader, and an inspired hawker of brave ideas, this canny and mystical, practical and prophetic man was one of the great forces of history.

Nevertheless, the contradictions implicit in his thinking make Columbus a magnificent puzzle. The ease with which he crossed an unexplored ocean and hit his target near the center time after time, and his ability not only as an instinctive deep-sea navigator but as a master of the shoals and reefs of inshore sailing—these stamp him as the greatest mariner of his day. The boldness with which he put into practice his idea that mariners could sail straight across the sea to Asia marks him as the most resolute theorist of his age, for while others had agreed in principle, no one else had dared attempt the feat. But with all this seemingly modern determination to test a hypothesis, there was in Columbus a stubbornness—it must be China!—and a self-deception—all that gold!—that cannot be accounted for entirely by the geographical naïveté that he inherited from the late-medieval world.

When, for example, he decided that the enormous volume of the Orinoco River could only issue from a continent, he was pursuing straightforward cause-and-effect reasoning of the kind that might be expected from a "Renaissance mind." But his subsequent declaration that the river flowed from the Earthly Paradise was far from empirical.

Some of his other conclusions were equally fuzzy. Sailing repeatedly across the Atlantic, he had become convinced that he was going uphill when going west, downhill when returning home. After leaving the Azores for the Antilles, "the ships," he noted, "went on rising smoothly towards the sky." Moreover, the weather became progressively warmer from east to west, confirming his belief that his ships were being gently lifted toward the sun. It followed, therefore, that the earth was not round, as was commonly believed, but pear-shaped, "having a raised projection for the stalk." The Terrestrial Paradise he placed "on the summit . . . of the stalk of a pear."

If this and other instances made Columbus appear part thinker, part mystic, it is because he was at heart a poet with a poet's faith in the existence of marvels that defies the bounds of logic. He loved the new theories about geography proclaimed by Italian scholars, and he had turned his back on the out-of-date, Jerusalem-centered maps of the Middle Ages. But he still believed that somewhere at the meeting of East and West was the Terrestrial Paradise, where man lived in heroic beauty and freedom, uncontaminated by Adam's fall; he wanted to find the way both to Cathay and to Paradise, and, by his own standards, he did.

Columbus started the train of events that led to modern America. In his wake Spaniards and foreigners in Spanish service, prompted by the Ad-miral's discoveries, set forth on successive journeys of reconnaissance. If the Spaniards had not explored America, others doubtless would have—but not so soon or so vigorously, and with vastly different consequences for the American continent and for Europe itself.

No other nation but Spain could have produced the conquistadors, those daring and ruthless soldiers of fortune. Without the conquistadors the Aztec and Inca empires would not have fallen so soon or so catastrophically, and Europe would not have been flooded with the precious metals that sluiced through Spain—a country that was ill equipped to use the wealth for constructive purposes. As a result of the almost unchecked flow of bullion, Europe experienced an economic revolution that was as important in determining the fortunes of nations as the actions of kings or lesser statesmen. Without Spain's dominance in the Caribbean, English seamen like Drake would not have been encouraged to try to intercept her treasure ships there, and thence take an increasing interest in the parts of America that were free from Catholic control. The power in Europe that Spain gained from her new possessions almost compelled the English to counteraction in the New World. Had Spain not become so threatening, there might have been no settlement in Virginia, no Pilgrim Fathers, no English-speaking North American colonies, no United States.

All this is speculation, but it is a fact that if Columbus had not existed, and if the discovery had been made by another man, at another time, the whole of American history would be different. Not only the language in which this book is read, but the sentiments of its readers, the quality of the life they lead owes something to Columbus. This makes him, however accidentally, however indirectly, one of the most influential men who have ever lived. It may make him the most influential man of all, excepting only the leaders of world religions.

A DUTCH CARTOGRAPHER, *dividers in hand, works amid charts, globe and other paraphernalia of his craft.*

THE CHART-MAKERS

As the epic journeys of the 15th and 16th Centuries began to transform Western man's view of the world, a demand arose for more accurate maps and charts. The fanciful geographies of antiquity—which pictured the earth as a single, interconnected land mass bordered by unknown seas—slowly gave way to surveys based on firsthand observations, aided by new navigational instruments. With the nations of Europe hungering to stake their claims in newly discovered lands, the mapping of earth and heavens became more than an aid to navigation; it was the key to empire. Thus, with increasing precision, coastlines were determined, sea routes charted, harbors sounded and the direction of auspicious winds carefully noted. Combining the artist's skill with the mathematician's knowledge of geometry, early cartographers patiently collated the records of mariners until, piece by piece, a true model of the earth's surface began to take shape.

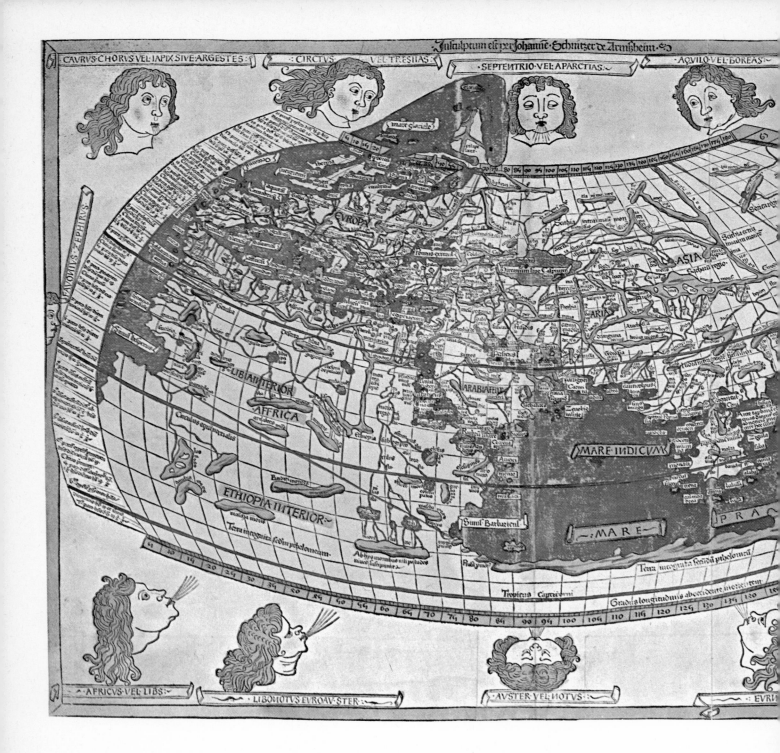

LEGACIES FROM THE ANCIENT WORLD

The richest single heritage the explorers had to draw on was the knowledge of the ancient Greeks. These early seafarers and astronomers of the Mediterranean had taken care to map their world and chart their heavens (right, below). Claudius Ptolemy's famous geographical works of the Second Century were still models for cartographers 1,300 years later (above). Though he badly underestimated the earth's size, Ptolemy popularized an early system of longitude and latitude, and pictured a round world—a view that 15th Century mariners confirmed as they began to range across the seas.

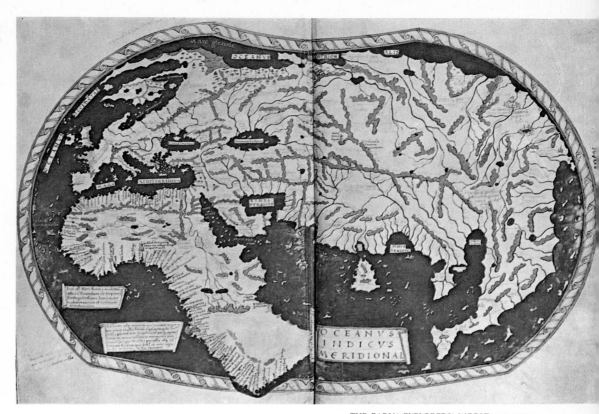

THE EARLY EXPLORERS' WORLD, *as seen in this late-15th Century map, greatly exaggerated the size of land masses at the expense of still-uncharted oceans. However it did reflect detailed, firsthand observations of the West African coast.*

TOLEMY'S WORLD *is re-created in this 1482 map printed in Germany. Dotted with mythical islands and mountains, it indicates the extent of the ancients' ignorance regarding Africa, the Indian Ocean and Asia.*

A CELESTIAL GLOBE *of the Second Century A.D. rests on the shoulders of Atlas. Carved on it are most of the 48 constellations identified by Ptolemy, reflecting a more complete knowledge of the heavens than men had of the earth.*

On the map, the following labels appear:

Circulus articus:

Oceanus occidentalis

Mare germanicus

Terra del Rey de portugall

has antilhas del Rey de castella

Esta he o marco entre castella e portugall

Os montes claros en affrica

da esta terra he decoberta p mādao del Rey de castella

Lixboa   Castello damina

Ilinha equinocialis:

Tropicus capricorn.

Mare oceanus:

Pollus antarticus:

KEYS TO THE OCEAN BARRIERS

"I gave the keys of those mighty barriers of ocean which were closed with such mighty chains," wrote Columbus. It was true: the most dramatic leap forward in man's concept of the world occurred as a result of his voyages. The map above, made in 1502, reveals a new understanding of the vastness of the earth. This remarkably detailed document is known as the Cantino map for the envoy who secretly commissioned its execution in Lisbon for the Duke of Ferrara, an Italian prince and map collector who was fascinated by the new Portuguese and Span-

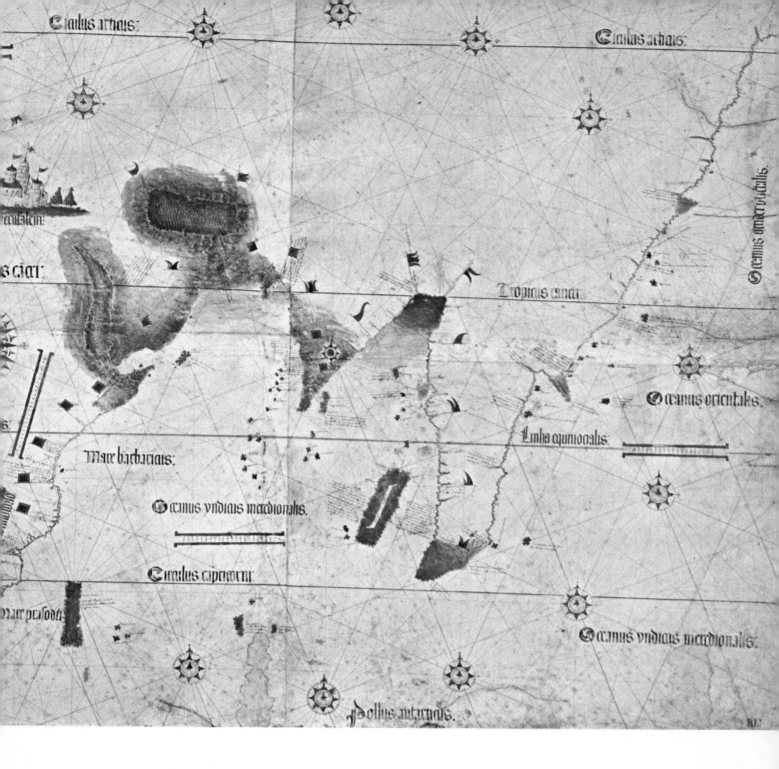

ish discoveries. A 19th Century collector found it hanging in a butcher shop in Modena.

Not only does the Cantino map depict the entire continent of Africa with precision, but India, although tapering too sharply toward the tip, has acquired its true peninsula shape as a result of further Portuguese explorations.

Most intriguing of all, however, is the outline of the New World. Columbus had brought home impressively accurate and detailed descriptions of the new lands—islands in the West Indies are shown, as well as the shoreline of present-day Venezuela, Guiana and Brazil. But the map also offers a tantalizing indication that there might have been clandestine expeditions in the wake of Columbus, in violation of the New World monopoly granted Spain by the Tordesillas Treaty Line *(far left)*, which divided the undiscovered world between Spain and Portugal. How else could the land beyond *Oceanus occidentalis (top left)* have been mapped 11 years before Ponce de Leon momentously announced his discovery of Florida?

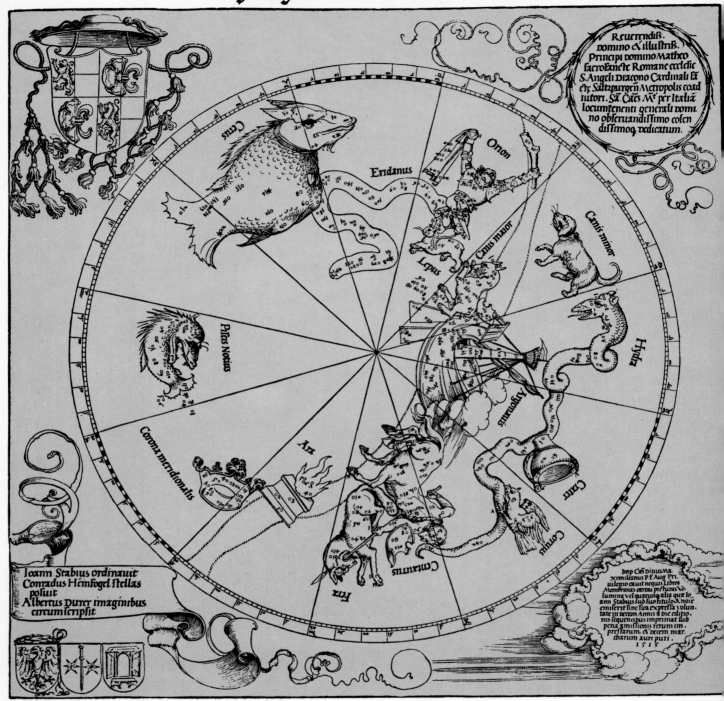

CHARTING THE HEAVENS

When Albrecht Dürer, working with two astronomers, artfully engraved the maps shown here—the first printed star charts—the skies of the Northern Hemisphere *(right)* were already crowded with the traditional gods, heroes, animals and objects that have represented the constellations since Greek and Roman times. Among them are Taurus, Gemini, Cancer, Leo, Scorpio, Pegasus, Hercules, Sagittarius and Andromeda.

Imagines cœli Septentrionales cum duodecim imaginibus zodiaci.

The age of discovery was to add much to this array. In 1515, when these woodcuts were published in Nuremberg, Spanish and Portuguese penetration of the southern latitudes had only just begun; no systematic study of the skies below the equator had yet been made. Thus, in the Dürer star charts, the southern portion of the heavens *(left)* is relatively devoid of constellations—although it actually has more stars than the northern half. The star clusters that later explorers discovered and named have the strong flavor of their travels in the south: Indus the Indian, Tucana the Toucan, Pavo the Peacock, Dorado the Goldfish, Apus the Bird of Paradise. Framing the array of mythological figures in the Northern Hemisphere are the four early astronomers—including Ptolemy *(upper right)*—whose works Dürer also drew upon to make these star maps.

67

A DECORATIVE CHART *made about 1527, five years after Magellan's voyage around the globe, displays two ships in the Indian and Pacific Oceans. Crossed with wind roses and rhumb lines used in navigation, it is framed by the faces of the four winds.*

SHOOTING A STAR *to fix his position, a French mariner uses an early navigating instrument which he has brought ashore. True sightings were difficult to make aboard wave-tossed vessels, which accounts for many of the inaccuracies in early maps.*

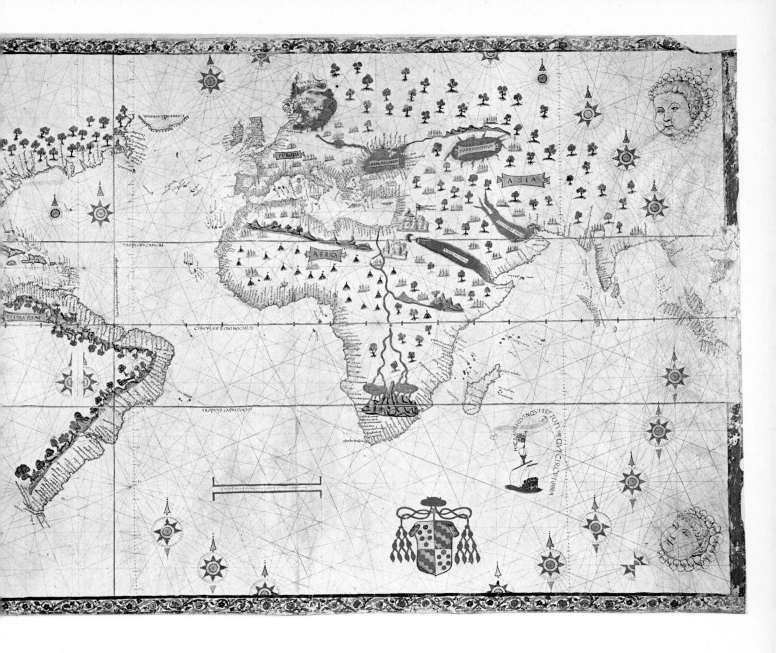

SHADOWY CONTOURS AND UNDISCOVERED LANDS

Despite the increasing knowledge with which map makers traced the coastlines of the world, vast regions of the earth, especially the interiors, remained uncharted. The map above, a product of Spain's map-making center at Seville, is typical of those published around the time of Magellan's circumnavigation of the globe. It offers a strikingly accurate picture of the Atlantic coastline from England to the Cape of Good Hope and from Labrador to the Strait of Magellan, as well as giving sharper definition to the East African coast. In its enlarged view of the world, however, the map also shows some notable gaps: the main bodies of North and South America are still missing, the Pacific is devoid of islands (including the continent of Australia), and the East Indies are only vaguely conceived.

A FLAT VIEW
OF A ROUND WORLD

The great technological advance in 16th Century map making began with the realization that a useful navigational chart would have to project the curved lines of the globe accurately onto the flat surface of the map which represented it. In order to lay down directions as straight lines, some parts of the sphere would have to be pulled out of shape. Since most maritime traffic plied the Temperate Zones, it was vital to keep these areas relatively undistorted.

After many earlier attempts had failed, Gerhardus Mercator, a Flemish scholar and cartographer, finally devised a useful solution. In this Mercator projection drawn by Willem Blaeu, a Dutch map maker, the extreme northern and southern regions are stretched beyond recognition while areas near the equator are in their proper proportion. To compensate for these distortions, two polar projections have been drawn at the corners of the map.

Blaeu's maps were not only among the most accurate of the period; they were by far the most lavishly produced. This one is sprinkled with ships to indicate the principal trade routes, and its borders are decorated with allegorical representations of the four elements *(left)*; the four seasons *(right)*; the sun, moon and planets *(top)* and the seven wonders of the world.

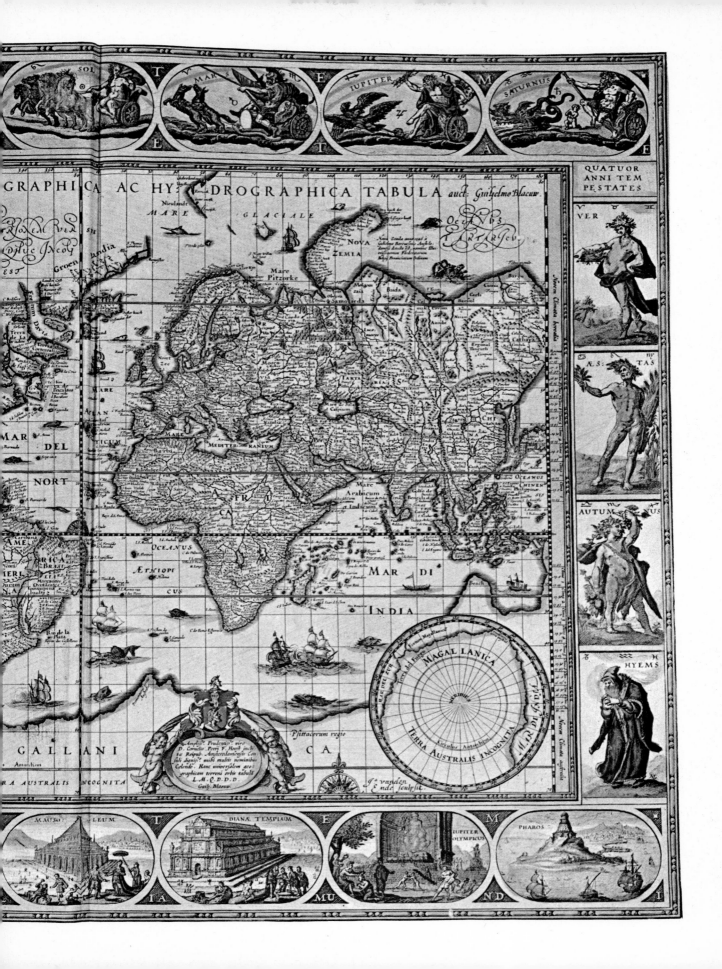

4

THE ART OF NAVIGATION

The essential things in exploring have always been to know where you want to go and to have the means of getting there. Intelligent men with a sense of purpose have explored only places they believed existed; they arrived only if they could persuade hardheaded people to put up the money to send them there. The nature of the destination has often been mysterious, its size and resources conjectural. But these are the only romantic aspects of exploration. Getting there involved danger, technical skill, patience and courage, but not—save by the hindsight of posterity—romance.

Storms, shipwrecks, hostile inhabitants were hazards common to all seafaring, even in European waters, and the explorer prepared himself as best he could to meet these mishaps. The real agonies suffered by Renaissance explorers arose from their encounters with the unforeseen. Renaissance explorers relied on charts of their time, and since these were gravely inaccurate, even the most capable leaders were often faced by a longer voyage without landfalls than they had bargained for. Their most common reaction was baffled alarm at finding sea—as in the South Atlantic and South Pacific—where they counted on finding land; or at finding land instead of the expected sea passages north of America and Asia. Almost always the unforeseen involved delay and its aftermath—food shortage and disease, extra weeks on the open ocean or months of imprisonment in the ice.

To put himself in the best condition to meet the unpredictable, a captain's first concern was to acquire strong, reliable craft for his expedition. Since there was no such thing as an exploration type of vessel during the Renaissance, he usually had to take what he could find among trading vessels lying idle at the time. These were mostly small and stubby, broad-beamed in proportion to their length, a shape that gave them strength and seaworthiness. Their bows lifted to waves coming head on, and their high sterns helped to keep them from being swamped by a following sea. But they paid for these advantages in reduced speed and the discomfort inherent in any vessel designed to bob over the waves rather than shear through them. Ships of this sort ranged from Columbus' *Niña*, about 70 feet long (roughly the size of some World

AN ARRAY OF ASTROLABES, *the elaborate "mathematical jewels" used by astronomers to determine time and latitude, represents over 750 years of star-charting. The oldest (third from top, far left) was made in Damascus or Baghdad about 830 A.D., the most recent (the 12-sided instrument to the right of it) in Prague in 1585. Navigators used cruder versions at sea.*

War II PT boats), to the 75-foot *Golden Hind*, which Sir Francis Drake took clear around the world. But vessels as small as the 20-ton *Gabriel*, in which Martin Frobisher crossed the North Atlantic, also gave good accounts of themselves. Big merchantmen, of 500 tons and more, were developed in the late 16th Century, under government auspices, to follow up the discoveries, to take settlers out and to bring back cargo. But from the point of view of safety, the little ships in which the initial discoveries were made probably had the edge.

In modern times there have been too many singlehanded crossings of the Atlantic in tiny boats to feel over-sentimental about the explorers' little craft that were sometimes alone on the oceans for months at a time. The hard lessons learned by medieval traders journeying from northern Europe to Spain across the Bay of Biscay, and by fishermen working the North Sea and the waters of Iceland had been incorporated in the design of Renaissance vessels. Ships that had ridden out gales in the English Channel in the 15th Century were ready to cope with gales off Cape Horn in the 16th. Later developments in shipbuilding enabled captains to sail faster and closer into head winds, but hardly enhanced the seaworthiness of their craft.

Nevertheless, the early vessels had their drawbacks. The fact that they could not sail close to the wind meant that far more laborious tacking (the zigzag course taken to move against a head wind) was needed than with later vessels. Adverse winds, however mild, could inordinately prolong voyages.

In a severe storm, a captain had to lower some or all sails and let the gale blow him where it would. Not until the introduction of better small sails in the 19th Century could ships ride out a storm with a fair chance of staying on course. But if foul weather made many goals unapproachable, if tempests caused sailors to overshoot their marks —as Dias was blown unwittingly clean past the

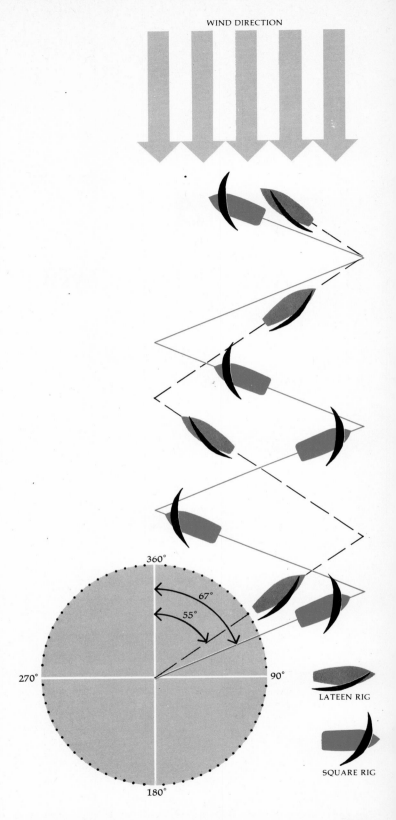

SAILING TO WINDWARD *became easier with the introduction of the triangular lateen sail, which enabled a ship to point within 55 degrees of the wind instead of only about 67 degrees, as with square sails. Thus the lateener could sail a shorter course to windward (black line) than the square-rigger (blue line).*

Cape of Good Hope to the edge of the Indian Ocean —other discoveries came about through the same accidents of squalls at sea. The Cape Verde Islands were discovered in 1456 by a vessel in Portuguese service fleeing from a storm. Japan was first sighted in 1542 by a ship buffeted past its destination on the Asian mainland by a typhoon. John Davis drifted under bare masts into the neighborhood of the Falkland Islands in 1592 while he was trying to make the Strait of Magellan.

Despite all the drawbacks of 15th Century vessels, the voyagers had craft that they, and their backers, could believe in. To increase their chances of success ships generally sailed in groups of two, three or four. From the beginning of the 16th Century, squadrons often consisted of various special-purpose vessels, including one ship that was faster than the others, to fetch help or to be first back home with news, and a larger storeship from which the smaller vessels could be reprovisioned.

For coastal explorations once the new land was reached, explorers needed small, shallow-draft vessels called pinnaces, equipped with oars for progress against head winds, or for going up rivers. These boats were usually taken along either as deck cargo or stored in pieces for later assembly overseas. Sometimes, however, they were constructed on the spot; much of the Central American coastline was explored by boats built in the West Indies. Although explorers could have used the small craft made by skilled native craftsmen, they rarely did so. Jacques Cartier, who used Indian canoes in Canada, is a notable exception, but he was one of the few early explorers to investigate minor waterways, where seagoing craft could not venture.

Once out of sight of land, the discoverers were at the mercy of their crude instruments, to help them plot a course and hold it, to keep some track of their progress on a chart and to estimate their positions. But celestial observation was in its in-fancy and usually unreliable. Modern ships pitch and roll, but their movement is trivial compared to the wallowing of a Renaissance vessel, and even today it takes some time to learn to get accurate sighting with a sextant. The early navigator had to brace himself against his ship's wallowing motion while he aligned the coarsely graded sights of his astrolabe or his cross-staff with the sun or a star; then he had to hold the sight while it was read against the scale of degrees. These were processes that did not make for a high degree of accuracy.

The theory was there, worked out by astronomers ashore and made available for seamen in a host of manuals. There were tables that explained how to measure and translate the angle between the horizon and the North Star or the noonday sun into degrees of latitude, in order to determine how far north or south of the equator the ship was. But few mariners had the mathematical knowledge, let alone the mathematical imagination, to use the tables properly. Moreover, celestial observations depend on knowing the exact time and there was no clock suitable for use at sea. Sailors relied on the half-hour or hourly sandglass until the mid-18th Century—and these, of course, had to be reset manually all during the voyage. During the 16th Century, methods of navigation were improved by men working in Seville, Lisbon and London, but the gap between theoretical knowledge and its application remained large, and so did the difference between the accuracy of observations made on land and at sea.

The most trustworthy instrument at sea was the compass; this the mariner used constantly. The compass had become accurate enough by about 1300 A.D. to allow ships to ply the Mediterranean and cross the Bay of Biscay even in winter, when visibility was poor. By 1380 the magnetized, north-pointing needle, attached to a card on which were marked the principal compass points, permitted the navigator to follow a course to within a few degrees. Columbus, whose celestial observations were often startlingly wrong (as when he located Moustique Bay in Haiti in the latitude of Wilmington, North Carolina, some 1,100 miles to the north), had the good sense not to trust his observations. He relied instead on his compass and on his shrewd estimates of the miles covered each day. As a navigational instrument the compass, too, had its drawbacks, for little was known about variation, the pull exerted on the compass by the earth's magnetic field; the difference between the compass needle's "north" and true north was worked out only by trial and error, voyage by voyage.

By and large, however, the compass was quite accurate as a navigational aid for voyagers who ventured beyond sight of the land. It was also valuable in mapping a coastline. From the end of the 13th Century, the compass had been used to make a series of portolans—pilotage manuals with illustrated charts of European coastlines, especially those of the Mediterranean and of France, Spain and Portugal. These books were an essential feature of the navigator's equipment, for they showed his destination and enabled him to plot each day's progress. The portolans of coastal European waters covered relatively small north-south distances as compared with the vast distances mapped on marine charts of the open seas. But the marine charts used the same cartographic principles as portolans and thereby created serious problems for mariners.

Since longitudes encircle the earth at right angles to the equator and converge at the Poles, the degree of separation between them decreases the farther they are from the equator. For a navigator charting his course across the vast and uncertain reaches of the Atlantic Ocean in the early 16th Century, the farther north his vessel was from the equator, the more difficult it became to mark an accurate east-west course because of the progressive variation in distance between longitudinal lines. The explanation of this confusion was clear enough when a world globe was available, but until well past the middle of the 16th Century map makers were baffled by the problem of correcting the discrepancy on a chart. Then in 1569 Gerhardus Mercator, a Flemish geographer, published a projection which gave mariners a much more accurate tool. It took time for navigators to learn how to use the new chart and as late as 1646 one expert complained: "I could wish all seamen would give over sailing by the false plain charts, and sail by Mercator's chart, which is according to the truth of navigation. But it is a hard matter to convince any of the old navigators."

The "old navigators" were of a traditionally conservative stamp, as are most seamen to this day. In the light of their misleading charts, their inaccurate instruments and the virtual impossibility of determining longitude at this period, there were good reasons why mariners clung to conservative methods of navigation, principally that of dead reckoning (while the origin of this term is in dispute, one explanation is that it is a contraction of the word "deduced" into "ded," misspelled "dead").

Dead reckoning, by no means a foolproof technique, involves estimating a position in terms of distance sailed along a known compass bearing. But to know how far a ship has sailed in a day requires knowing its speed, and the log line, a simple speed-measuring device, did not come into general use until the late 1500s. Before that and, indeed, well after, mariners relied on their knowledge of how their vessel ran under different weather conditions, a knowledge gained by watching how rapidly patches of weed or pieces of flotsam fall astern. During the four-hour watches into which a ship's working day has traditionally been divided, estimates of speed were made for each of the eight half-hours of a watch. With following winds, the totals gave a reasonable estimate of how far the ship had run during

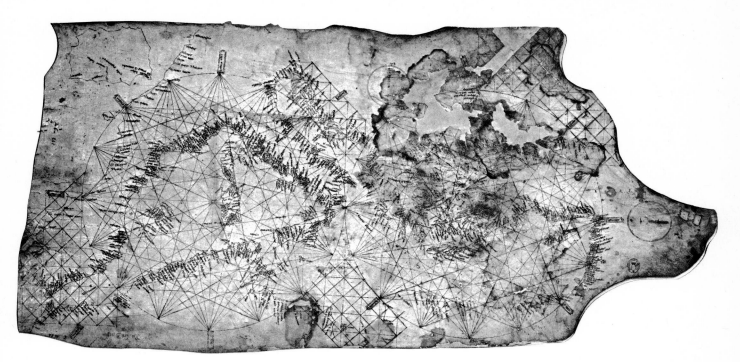

A SHEEPSKIN CHART, *the "Carte Pisane," is the oldest surviving map of the early portolan type. Used by 13th Century Mediterranean pilots, it provided a network of rhumb lines representing 16 "half-winds" or bearings. To chart his course, a pilot laid a ruler between his point of departure and his destination, then sought the bearing most nearly parallel to it.*

the day, though unsuspected currents could affect a judgment of speed, and also of direction.

With contrary winds, which made extensive tacking necessary, the dead-reckoning estimate became much more tricky. Traverse boards, on which successive changes of heading could be plotted, gave navigators some help in figuring how much forward progress had been made during the zigzag tacks. But even then practical experience was required to make the proper allowances for the leeway, or sideward slippage, on each zig and zag. All in all, it is not surprising that seagoing navigators —ignoring a chorus of baffled vituperation from shore-based experts—trusted more to instinct shaped by knowledge of their own ship than to books written by landlubbers. At sea, as in love, it is often better to back a hunch than obey the books.

Generally speaking, a skilled mariner would "sail latitudes"; that is, he sailed south or north until celestial observation fixed his latitude, and then he headed east or west until he hit land. The technique was later summed up in the direction for sailing from Europe to the West Indies: "south till the butter melts, and then due west." Given the uncertain state of knowledge, it is easy to understand why Vasco da Gama, although well stocked with charts and navigational instruments, devoted great pains to securing a pilot with personal knowledge of the Indian Ocean.

It is easy to understand, too, how much mariners depended on their observation of weed and flotsam, and on the behavior of winds and fishes, for these were often their only indication that their landfall was near. Excerpts from the detailed instructions Pero de Queiros wrote for his Pacific voyage of 1606 indicate the importance of the signs: "If the sea appears greasy, with leaves of trees, grass, herbs, wood, branches, palm nuts, and other things which the waves carry from the shores and rivers send down when in flood, it is a sign of land being near.

... If the birds that may be met with are piqueros, ducks, widgeons, gulls, estopegados, terns, sparrow-hawks, flamingos or siloricos, it is a sign that land is very near; but if there are only boobies so much care is not necessary, because these birds are found far from land. . . . If the sea is of any other color than the ordinary one of the ocean where there is great depth, namely, dark blue, it is necessary to exercise care, and much more if at night the sea should be heard to make sounds greater than is usual."

When a captain suspected, from one or another of these signs, that he was nearing land, he made constant use of the sounding line, a cord weighted with a lead plummet. With the line he could measure depths of as much as 200 fathoms (1,200 feet) and successive soundings would indicate whether the sea bottom was shelving up toward a coastline still over the horizon. In addition, the nature of the bottom could be examined from the fragments that lodged in a tallow-filled hole at the base of the lead weight. Careful records were kept of sounding depths and bottom samples, for these, together with graphic descriptions of landmarks sighted, would help a mariner to retrace his earlier voyage on a subsequent trip. In time, collections of navigators' records were assembled into pilotage books, invaluable to the captain approaching a harbor he had never before visited.

No subject was of greater interest to sailors than the pattern of the great ocean winds—and here the shore-based experts were of no help at all. Mariners had to find out for themselves that the seas are divided into certain zones in which the trade winds blow steadily in certain directions, and others—the doldrums—in which the air is still for months at a time. They also had to learn that the zones change with the seasons. Slowly a map of the invisible winds was superimposed on the map of the coasts and islands.

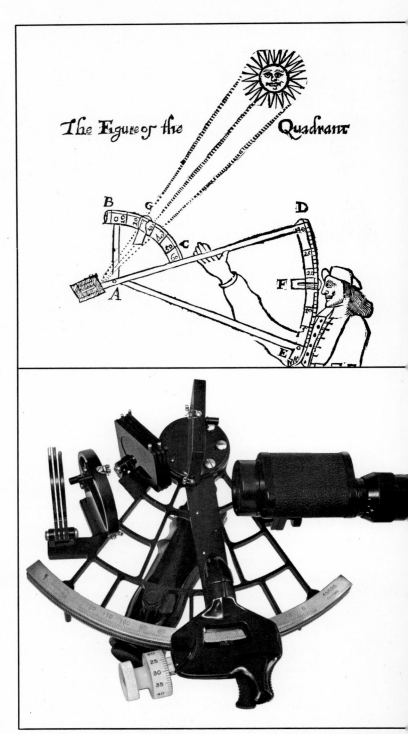

SHOOTING THE SUN *with a 16th Century backstaff, or English quadrant (top), as w*
a modern sextant (bottom), helped mariners determine the altitude of the sun abo
the horizon to fix a ship's latitude. This quadrant (so named because degrees w
marked on a quarter-circle) was advanced for its day, but was cumbersome. The co
pact, accurate sextant (which uses a sixth of a circle) was first developed around 17.

The best route came to be seen not as a straight-forward course between two points, but along the lengthy, curving corridors swept by the trades. From Spain to the West Indies ships followed the arc of the northeast trade wind which blew them from the Canaries to the Lesser Antilles in about a month. To return to Spain in winter, they beat their way north, against head winds, until past Bermuda, and then relaxed for the rest of the trip home on the endless belt of the westerlies.

Traffic patterns in the Indian Ocean were dictated by the seasonal reversal in direction of the monsoon, described by one traveler as "a path of wind that continues to blow for three or four months unceasingly, never letting up or changing." To get from Europe to India a ship had to leave the Cape of Good Hope by early summer in order to be carried across by the southwest monsoon. This "summer monsoon" locked up all ships in the west coast harbors of India till late autumn. Then the "winter monsoon," blowing from the northeast, released the waiting vessels and blew them back to Africa.

The discovery of the wind routes was a painfully slow process that was accomplished by ships thrusting and turning against the seemingly inexhaustible pressure of the moving air until at last the puzzle was solved. It was not until 1565, for example, that mariners who had vainly sought favorable winds for an eastward passage from the East Indies discovered that they had to go as far north as the 42nd parallel to find them.

The learning process was further slowed by the reluctance of governments to publicize knowledge that might aid the mariners of rival nations. By imposing secrecy, governments also ensured that their own merchants, who wanted to trade in the new lands, would have to work through the Crown, and thus be subject to its financial control. King John II had initiated this policy in Portugal in the days of Henry the Navigator, and he made the be-trayal of secrets of discovery punishable by death.

Nonetheless the stories, in whole or in part, always leaked out. Pilots and captains worked now for one government, now for another, and they took their information with them from job to job. Sailors and merchants gossiped in foreign ports, as ex-patriates always do. There was also a persistent clandestine traffic in charts; the Cantino chart of 1502, the earliest surviving record of Portuguese discoveries, was smuggled by Alberto Cantino to the Duke of Ferrara. Like all Italian princes, the Duke was alert to the threat posed to Italian domination of the spice trade by Da Gama's circumnavigation of Africa.

By the late 16th Century the conspiracy of silence was breaking down, a process aided by the efforts of Richard Hakluyt, an English clergyman and geographer who collected and published both accounts of voyages and minutely detailed sailing directions for various parts of the globe. Although he was genuinely anxious to spread knowledge, Hakluyt also hoped to awaken Englishmen to the glory to be obtained by expansion overseas.

Hakluyt untiringly assembled information, and he made excellent use of the records that captains were instructed to keep. When Arthur Pet and Charles Jackman, for example, set off in 1580 to find the northeast passage to China, they were told: "When you come to have sight of any coast or land whatsoever . . . set the same with your sailing compass how it bears off you, noting your judgment how far you think it from you, drawing also the form of it in your book." They were to repeat such observations on different bearings, describing and drawing the landmarks, "unto the which you may give apt names at your pleasure." Whenever they landed, they were to make detailed notes of the nature of the country, its products, its people and what they wanted as trade goods from England.

When an expedition was ready to set off on a

voyage of discovery, the commander, usually called the captain-general, summoned the ships' captains and pilots to a meeting, and established the rules of the journey. These responsible officers were exhorted to keep detailed logs and make regular sights of the sun, the North Star or the Southern Cross. They were to hold regular religious services, forbid gambling and, according to Sebastian Cabot's order, make sure that there was no swearing, "nor communication of ribaldry, filthy tales, or ungodly talk to be suffered in the company of any ship." Unless sailors have changed greatly, these rules were probably taken with a pinch of salt.

The regulations for maintaining formation on the high seas by day, by night or in fog were taken more seriously, for loss of contact with the other vessels could lead to disaster. The instructions dealing with signals were especially thorough. In fog these were given by blasts on a trumpet or a horn, by the beating of a drum or by the firing of a gun. On clear days orders to alter course or lower sails were given by one or more flags; on clear nights lanterns were used. With these means, it was possible to create a rudimentary code for sending and acknowledging such signals as: come aboard for conference; enemy sail; I am in distress; come near, I want to speak to you.

The captain-general also gave his captains sealed orders for rendezvous in case they did lose one another. Queiros, for instance, on his voyage westward across the Pacific from Peru in 1606, told any captain who became separated to make for the hazily known island of Santa Cruz and wait there for three months. "If, by chance the other ships do not arrive," the instructions continued, "the captain, before he departs, is to raise a cross, and at the foot of it, or of the nearest tree, he is to make a sign on the trunk, to be understood by him who next arrives, and to bury a jar with the mouth closed with tar and containing a narrative of all that has hap-

pened and of his intentions." This use of buried messages began early in the 16th Century, and it is not unlikely that it gave rise to many tales of mysterious maps and buried treasure, such as the one immortalized in Robert Louis Stevenson's *Treasure Island.*

Under the best of circumstances it was hard to predict the length of voyages. Columbus on his fourth expedition took 21 days to come the 3,000 miles from Grand Canary to Martinique, but this was in exceptionally favorable weather. Magellan, going west, crossed the Pacific in 98 days; the eastward crossing could take as much as six months. Sir Francis Drake was at sea for 54 days between the Cape Verde Islands and Brazil, a distance of 1,600 miles. The trip from Lisbon to Goa, crossing well-charted seas and utilizing favorable winds, averaged seven months. An Italian traveler, writing in about 1600, assured his readers that in going around the world "one does not put in more than sixteen and one half months of sailing."

Conditions of life aboard during these lengthy voyages were appalling, not only by modern standards but by the standards of the time for life on shore. All the ships leaked; even with regular use of the pumps, water was constantly sloshing in the bilge which was further fouled by the casual sanitary habits of the age. Roaches and rats swarmed everywhere. No sleeping quarters were provided, save perhaps for the master and pilot: ordinary seamen slept on or below deck wherever they could find room. There was no waterproof clothing.

Explorers' ships were less crowded than those that followed, for follow-up vessels were jammed with soldiers, settlers and merchants in addition to the crew. But the later travelers at least were following known routes and knew the duration of their voyage, within the limits imposed by wind and sea.

Sheer discomfort and stench probably did not

AN ALL-PURPOSE COMPASS ROSE *from a 1596 sailor's manual showed navigators two systems for describing a ship's course—by degrees (inner circle) and by compass points (outer names). Sundial markings (outer circle) were intended for telling time. The fleur-de-lis and cross distinguished north and east.*

mean much to those who were used to the sea as traders or fishermen. But the voyages of discovery created major problems in the way of food supply. In part this reflected the large number of men needed to handle the sails of the early exploring vessels and for whom stores of food that would last for the whole voyage had to be carried. But there were other factors that added to the difficulties: the tendency of grain and ship's biscuit to become sour or to swarm with weevils; the speed with which even the best-made wine or water casks sprang leaks under the continual lurching of the ship.

Food problems limited a captain's ability to sail where he chose and induced him to proceed by indirect, island-hopping paths whenever he had a choice, rather than by more direct and often less dangerous courses. Sometimes the captains assumed great risks to ensure an adequate supply of food for their crews. For example, when John Davis was attempting to make a passage through the treach-

erous Strait of Magellan in 1591, he sent a landing party ashore in small boats with instructions to kill and salt the penguins which nested there, for the preserved meat would be a valuable supplement to the ship's provisions on the journey's next leg.

What a shortage of food could mean is grimly described in the remarkably detailed chronicle of Magellan's Pacific crossing: "We ate only old biscuit reduced to powder, and full of grubs, and stinking from the dirt which the rats had made on it when eating the good biscuit, and we drank water that was yellow and stinking. We also ate the ox hides which were under the main-yard so that the yard should not break the rigging . . . also the sawdust of wood, and rats."

As this account indicates, the food not only ran short, but went bad. Shipboard menus consisted of dried or salted meat, salted fish, biscuit, rice, dried peas, cheese, onions, garlic, oil, vinegar, water and wine. From the evidence of the records, seamen

VICTUALS FOR VOYAGING

When a ship's captain of the early 17th Century left port he brought on board supplies such as those listed below, calculated to feed 190 men for three months before rotting food, starvation and scurvy took their toll. As provisions ran out, he hoped for a landfall so he could restock with local delicacies such as breadfruit, yams and penguin meat.

8,000 POUNDS OF SALT BEEF

2,800 POUNDS OF SALT PORK

A FEW BEEF TONGUES

600 POUNDS OF HABERDINE (SALT COD)

15,000 BROWN BISCUITS

5,000 WHITE BISCUITS

30 BUSHELS OF OATMEAL

40 BUSHELS OF DRIED PEAS

1½ BUSHELS OF MUSTARD SEED

1 BARREL OF SALT

100 POUNDS OF SUET

1 BARREL OF FLOUR

11 FIRKINS (SMALL WOODEN CASKS) OF BUTTER

1 HOGSHEAD (LARGE CASK) OF VINEGAR

10,500 GALLONS OF BEER

3,500 GALLONS OF WATER

2 HOGSHEADS OF CIDER

Captain's Stores:

CHEESE, PEPPER, CURRANTS, CLOVES, SUGAR, AQUA VITAE, GINGER, PRUNES, BACON, MAR-MALADE, ALMONDS, CINNAMON, WINE, RICE

seem to have eaten about 3,500 calories a day, a perfectly adequate diet if it had been consistently available. Men in the Renaissance ate meals we should think dull. They had little meat and their choice depended on the season rather than on any sense of connoisseurship. Eating at sea swung from frugality during voyages to gluttonous orgies after making a landfall, a pattern that corresponded exactly to eating habits ashore. The difference for the sailor lay in the terrible quality of the food during the times of scarcity: the putrefying water; the fresh food petering out after a few days; then a diet unhealthily salty; then a time when even salted and dried provisions turned into a slimy mess, undulating with worms.

On a long trip, sailors relied on rains to replenish the water supply. Pero de Queiros is notable for using a primitive furnace to distill fresh water from the ocean; generally, however, water was collected during rainstorms—in buckets or as it dripped from heavy mats hung from the rigging. But when the rains failed there was no other source; there are instances of crews that were reduced to drinking their own urine.

Disease was rife on long journeys, and with good reason. Sailors ate a minimum of fresh vegetables; they were cramped and crowded, infested with fleas and lice, often drenched for days on end. While clean salt water slipped below the keel and fresh air blew over the decks, the crew was all too likely to be literally rotting with scurvy.

The logbooks talk of various kinds of fever, sometimes of plague; but scurvy, caused by vitamin C deficiency, was the occupational disease of deep-sea mariners. A voyage to India was considered favored if only one out of every five men died of scurvy. Though the disease is popularly associated with the tropics, it attacked seamen in subpolar waters with equal virulence.

Horrific contemporary descriptions tell us what

the disease was like: "It rotted all my gums," wrote one sufferer, "which gave out a black and putrid blood. My thighs and lower legs were black and gangrenous, and I was forced to use my knife each day to cut into the flesh in order to release this black and foul blood. I also used my knife on my gums, which were livid and growing over my teeth. . . . When I had cut away this dead flesh and caused much black blood to flow, I rinsed my mouth and teeth with my urine, rubbing them very hard. . . . And the unfortunate thing was that I could not eat, desiring more to swallow than to chew. . . . Many of our people died of it every day, and we saw bodies thrown into the sea constantly, three or four at a time. For the most part they died with no aid given them, expiring behind some case or chest, their eyes and the soles of their feet gnawed away by the rats."

We know less about the lighter side of life on board. Some men read, but little is known about the books they took along apart from a story of missionaries throwing chivalrous romances overboard and pressing religious tracts into the unwilling seamen's hands instead. The ship's musicians were doubtless employed to amuse the ship's company as well as to give signals. In the late 16th Century, Crossing the Line (the equator) was already marked by the horseplay that continues to this day. But the more common antidotes to boredom were the forbidden gambling, a daily religious service and, on ships of Catholic countries, the celebration of feast days with some semblance of an actual feast, weather and stores permitting.

On first arriving at a strange land, it was important to make a good impression—usually compounded equally of threat and reassurance—on the inhabitants. So, if they had time and energy, the crew dressed their ship with banners, the musicians struck up, guns were fired and the captain appeared on deck in his best clothes, sword at side.

Sometimes the voyagers had the advantage of being thought magical. Certain Caribbean Indians considered Columbus to be a god; West African natives called the first Portuguese ships great birds; Brazilian Indians believed that Magellan's pinnaces were born from his ships when they were let down into the water, and that when they were alongside they were being suckled by their mothers.

At least at the outset, every effort was made to placate the local inhabitants for it was necessary to obtain food and information, and this could be done most efficiently if the natives were friendly. Beads and little jingling bells were handed out, European hats were exchanged for headdresses of feathers or fur, chiefs were shown over the ships and regaled with European food. To gain information about objects of value, especially gold, natives were invited—or forced—on board. Sebastian Cabot instructed captains that prisoners were "to be well entertained, used, and apparelled, to be set on the land to the intent that he or she may allure others to draw nigh to show the commodities, and if the person taken may be made drunk with your beer or wine, you may know the secrets of his heart."

Attempts to make friends were not always successful. Columbus once ordered his young sailors to dance to the rhythm of a drum in order to attract some Indians who were lying some way off the ship in a large canoe. The Indians thought it was a war dance, however, and began shooting arrows.

Communication was the great difficulty. Sign language was sometimes helpful, sometimes not. Pedro Alvares Cabral gained the impression that Brazil was an island in this way, and Alvise da Cadamosto turned back from West Africa in despair because he could not understand what the natives were trying to tell him. Voyagers to the Indian Ocean, an Arabic-speaking trading area, could take interpreters with them who had learned the language from Moors resident in Spain and Portugal.

Elsewhere the natives were usually taught the language of their visitors, and it became a regular policy to take some of them home, forcibly if necessary, and train them as interpreters for later voyages. Other captives, after indoctrination, were returned to their own country for propaganda purposes. It was hoped that they would tell their chiefs about the wealth and power of Europe, the advantages of trading with it, and the dangers of resisting the demands of Europeans.

The Portuguese added a second measure: they dumped convicts (whose death sentences were commuted for this purpose) on newly discovered shores to learn the local language, plant European seeds and see whether European animals could flourish in new lands. Theoretically, the convicts were also to try to convert the natives to Christianity. The hope was that future voyages would find congenial outposts of Europe on the fringe of savage and exotic shores. The experiment was to some extent a success, and many ships' companies were cheered to receive a familiar welcome after the dragging monotony of their voyage. More frequently, however, the involuntary castaway was found to have gone happily native rather than to have created a little bit of Europe in the wilds.

The discoverers usually returned to their ships at night, but sometimes, while their ships were being overhauled, or to enjoy the hospitality of a trusted chief and his village, they slept on shore. There they discovered such disadvantages as mosquitoes. Weary sailors benefited, however, from fresh food and local herbal remedies, for almost every ship landed with men suffering from disease or some wound received while handling the ship in a storm.

Certain remedies, while effective, were not suited to adoption at home. When the adventurer Philip von Huten, for instance, was wounded in a brush with natives in South America, "an old slave was dressed in the German Knight's armour and placed on his horse, and, while in this position, an Indian wounded him in the same way that the Omagua had wounded Von Huten. Thus, by cutting the old slave up, they discovered the direction of Von Huten's wound, and cured him."

After caring for his ship and its crew, finding out all he could from the natives, taking his latitude and bringing his log up to date, a captain-general in a newly discovered land had one more duty: to take formal possession of it for his country. Conventions of uncertain origin governed this rite, whose form was usually explained in his sailing instructions. The Portuguese erected their inscribed stone pillars. In Mexico, the Spanish conquistador Hernando Cortes, acting without instructions, "took possession for his Majesty by drawing his sword and making three cuts in a huge tree . . . proclaiming that if anyone should object, he would defend his action with his sword and shield." The English discoverers of Elizabethan times set up the royal standard, or made piles of stones to warn later voyagers that someone had preceded them.

Most famous of all such gestures was that of Drake on his landing north of San Francisco. "At our departure hence," wrote one of his companions, "our general set up a monument of our being there, as also of her Majesty's right and title to the same, namely a plate, nailed upon a fair great post, whereupon was engraved her Majesty's name, the day and the year of our arrival there, with the free giving up of the province and people unto her Majesty's hands, together with her Highness' picture and arms in a piece of sixpence of current English money under the plate, whereunder was also written the name of our general." The recent discovery of this little plate (about the authenticity of which there is still some doubt) brings home poignantly the days when men of high courage and great seamanship sailed halfway around the world to claim lands far vaster than their own.

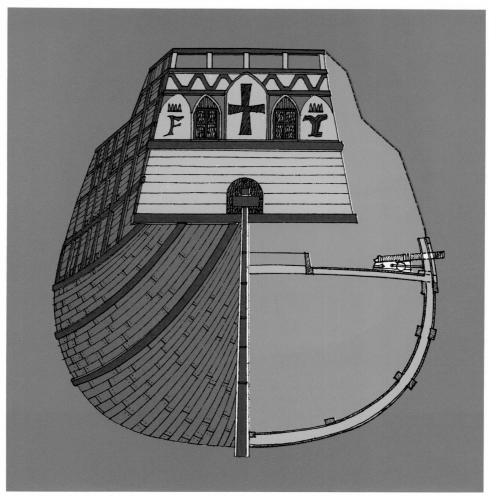

"SANTA MARIA'S" full, beamy hull is revealed in this stern view. Her cannon fired from the main deck.

SHIPS AND GEAR

Between 800 and 1500 the sailing vessel grew up. What had been an undecked open boat driven by one clumsy sail of leather or wool developed into a multi-masted, stern-ruddered goods carrier driven by several sails made of lighter, more manageable flax. Size and cargo capacity more than doubled; the canvas tarpaulin used to shelter the goods gave way to permanent wooden decks. The side rudder, which came out of the water when the ship rolled, was replaced by a rudder in the stern which was more easily handled and turned the ship faster. The single heavy sail was divided into five or six smaller, more easily handled units. Bow and stern were built up into "castles" from which marines could shoot down onto an enemy deck during naval battles; they also protected against pirates and mutinies within the ship's own crew. The overall result: a sturdy little vessel that could go anywhere and defend itself in any company.

THE EUROPEAN SHIP EVOLVES

European ships followed two lines of development, one in the north and one in the Mediterranean. As early as 800 A.D., the Vikings were using a long slender clinker-built vessel, the *knorr*, with a single square sail, for trade between Scandinavia and Iceland. Actually it was not unlike an enormous double-ended rowboat, steered by an oar at one side. It was swift and seaworthy, and thus capable of long ocean voyages; however its cargo capacity was small. By 1200 the

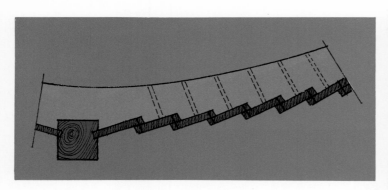

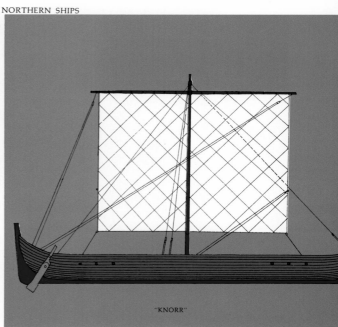

"KNORR"

NORTHERN SHIPS *were clinker-built; that is, their planking overlapped like siding on a house. The reason was simple; the northerners had not invented the saw. Unable to cut timbers with precise ends and compelled to use rough-edged lumber hand-cut with adzes, the Scandinavians adopted overlapping clinker construction and achieved surprisingly good results. Clinker planking proved stronger than carvel planking (below), so shipbuilders could use lighter framing. Clinkers also made better joints with less caulking. But there was one fatal flaw: on ships longer than 100 feet, joining problems became insuperable. In 1418, Henry V of England launched the super-clinker "Gracedieu," 180 feet long. Unseaworthy, it floated around for years until it burned down.*

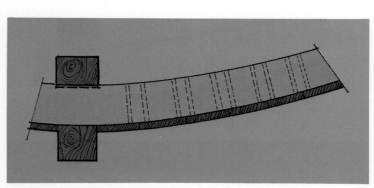

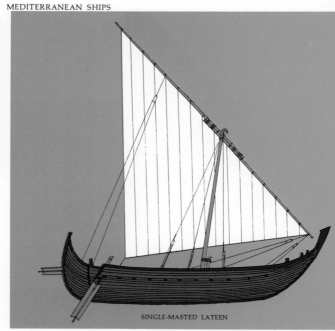

SINGLE-MASTED LATEEN

SOUTHERN SHIPS *were carvel-built; that is, their smooth-sided planks were fitted edge to edge over a frame with caulking in between. The southerners could do this because they had saws and could turn out square-cut planks. However, carvel planking required a strong inside frame. While the northern ship was basically solid planking with an added frame, the southern ship was basically a solid frame with added planking. Moreover, the southern carvel types suffered a serious drawback: they were difficult to make tight and water seeped in. But they enjoyed an overriding advantage: they could be built to any length. In 1853 the longest wooden clipper ever constructed, the carvel-built "Great Republic," 335 feet long, was launched in the U.S.*

knorr was operating all over northern Europe, and had become shorter and more heavy-bodied, reflecting its greater use for short-haul commerce. Small castles for fighting were added at bow and stern. By 1350 the hull had changed again. It was higher yet and broader, and now had a stern rudder and a distinct bow. Castles were an integral part of the hull design, and a tiny one for bowmen was put atop the mast.

In the Mediterranean, the lateener was chunkier than the *knorr*. Cargo carrying was important in the populous and relatively sheltered waters in which it operated. Also important was the ability to sail to windward, which lateen sail provided. By 1200 the lateener had also become heavier. It sprouted castles and two strongly stayed masts instead of one. By 1350 the northern type had penetrated the Mediterranean and the two traditions combined in the carrack, a stout square-rigged ship with a lateen-rigged mizzenmast.

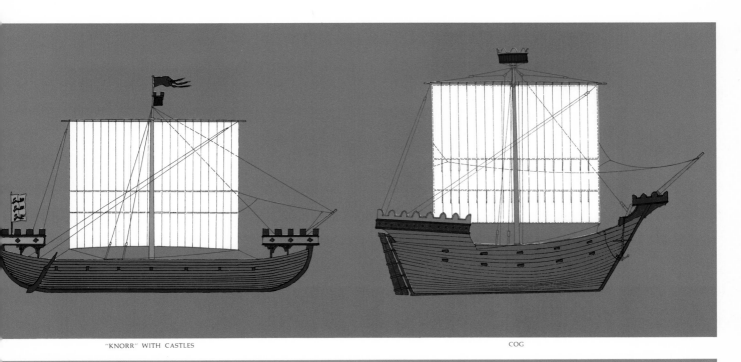

"KNORR" WITH CASTLES   COG

DOUBLE-MASTED LATEEN   CARRACK

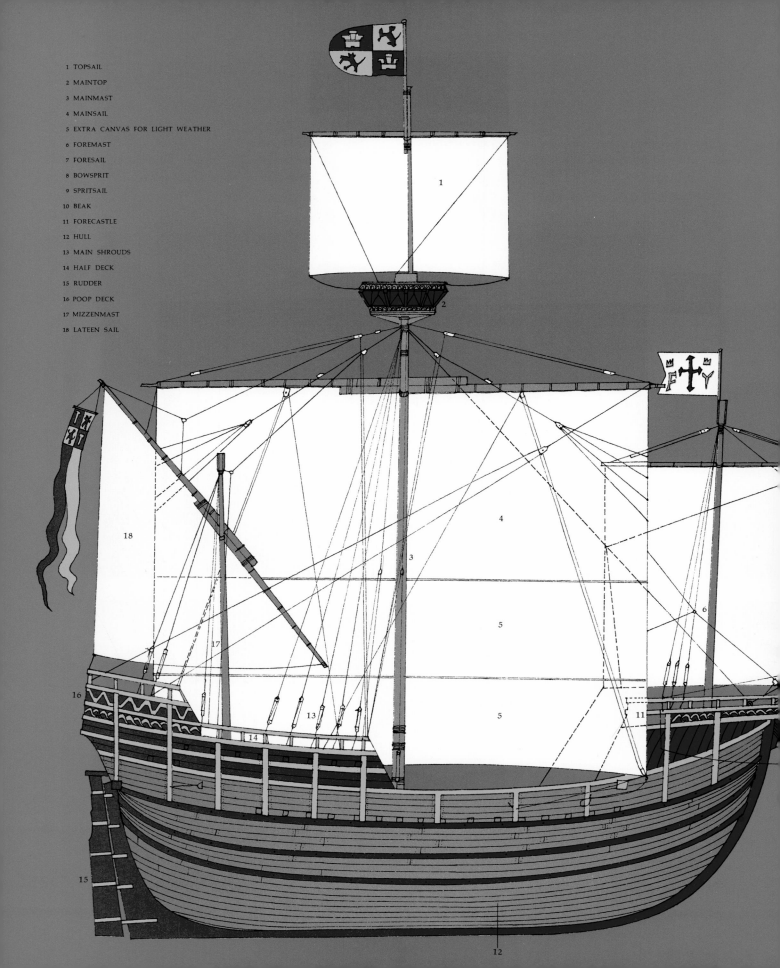

1 TOPSAIL

2 MAINTOP

3 MAINMAST

4 MAINSAIL

5 EXTRA CANVAS FOR LIGHT WEATHER

6 FOREMAST

7 FORESAIL

8 BOWSPRIT

9 SPRITSAIL

10 BEAK

11 FORECASTLE

12 HULL

13 MAIN SHROUDS

14 HALF DECK

15 RUDDER

16 POOP DECK

17 MIZZENMAST

18 LATEEN SAIL

A CLOSE LOOK AT THE "SANTA MARIA"

No one knows exactly what Columbus' flagship was like, but these drawings incorporate all the knowledge that does exist, with other details added from vessels of the period. We do know that the *Santa María* was a small carrack of about 150 tons' burden. Her length was 75 feet, her beam 25 feet and her draft 6 feet. She had a rounded bow and wide shoulders tapering aft—the "mackerel shape" of hull popular in the 17th Century. She was three-masted, and had five sails. Her mainsail was much the largest, and produced almost all her driving power, the others being used largely for trimming. During the following century the mainsail would shrink in size compared to the other sails. The foremast would get much taller and would eventually sprout another sail on top of the foresail. The maze of ropes shown is partly permanent rigging to hold the masts in place. These were made of hemp and stretched a great deal; consequently the rigger or boatswain had to spend a great deal of his time going around and around the ship tightening them up. The other ropes were for handling the sails: for tilting the yards up and down, for swinging them back and forth, for trimming the bottoms of the sails, and for bunching them up against the yards when the captain wanted them furled. Furling instead of lowering a sail to the deck, as is done in modern sailboats, was a necessity because the yardarm from which the sail hung was so heavy. Once hoisted into place, the yard was not lowered again except in emergencies.

All this made the *Santa María* a good average ship of her day, but Columbus did not think so. He labeled her a "dull sailer and unfit for discovery." Her deep draft was unsuited to nosing around among reefs and in shallow island waters, and on Christmas Day, 1492, she ran aground off Hispaniola and had to be abandoned.

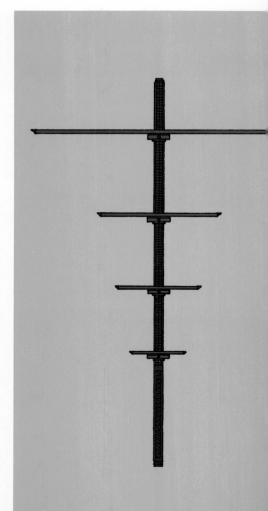

THE CROSS-STAFF *was fitted to take four movable crosspieces at right angles. Selecting a crosspiece, the sailor aimed it so that it lined up with the sun at its top and the horizon at its bottom. The distance of the crosspiece from the eye showed the sun's altitude.*

AIDS FOR NAVIGATORS

To make his way about in the oceans of the world, the early mariner had to know—as he still does—his latitude and longitude. Latitude, his north-south position, was theoretically easy to figure by reference to the sun. Metal discs called astrolabes had been in use for nearly 2,000 years. But they were developed by astronomers, and were not suited to use at sea. To get a correct reading from the heaving deck of a small ship was next to impossible, and astrolabes often produced errors of many hundreds of miles. This practical problem led to the development of the cross-staff *(right)*, a handier device for quickly measuring solar angles. Longitude requires accurate timepieces, and on long early voyages sailors forgot to turn the sandglass or turned it too soon. The best the mariner could do was measure his speed several times a day and guess at the number of miles he had traveled each day.

SHIP'S SPEED *was calculated by tossing a wood chip off the bow and timing it to the stern. Later the chip was tied to a knotted line and thrown over. Relating the knots that slipped through his fingers to elapsed time gave the sailor the ship's speed—in knots.*

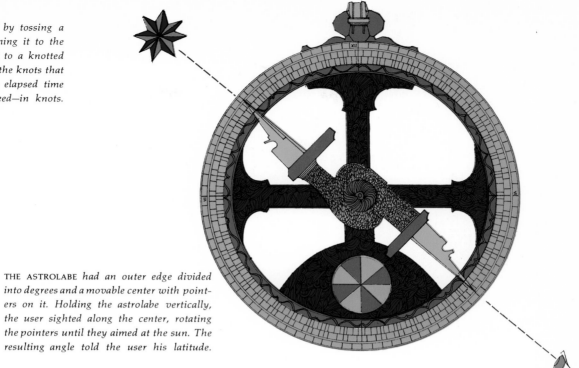

THE ASTROLABE *had an outer edge divided into degrees and a movable center with pointers on it. Holding the astrolabe vertically, the user sighted along the center, rotating the pointers until they aimed at the sun. The resulting angle told the user his latitude.*

1 MAINMAST
2 MAIN DECK
3 LONGBOAT
4 FORECASTLE
5 FOREMAST
6 BOWSPRIT
7 BEAK
8 SAILMAKERS
9 ANCHOR WINDLASS
10 ANCHOR LINES
11 LADDER
12 BOATSWAIN'S STORES
13 GUN DECK
14 CANNON
15 GALLEY
16 ROCK BALLAST

17 WATER CASKS
18 BEER CASKS
19 SHIP'S STORES
20 RUDDER
21 TILLER
22 WHIPSTAFF
23 BINNACLE
24 HELMSMAN
25 OFFICERS' BUNKS
26 GREAT CABIN
27 PILOT'S CABIN
28 POOP DECK
29 MIZZENMAST
30 HALF DECK
31 CAPSTAN

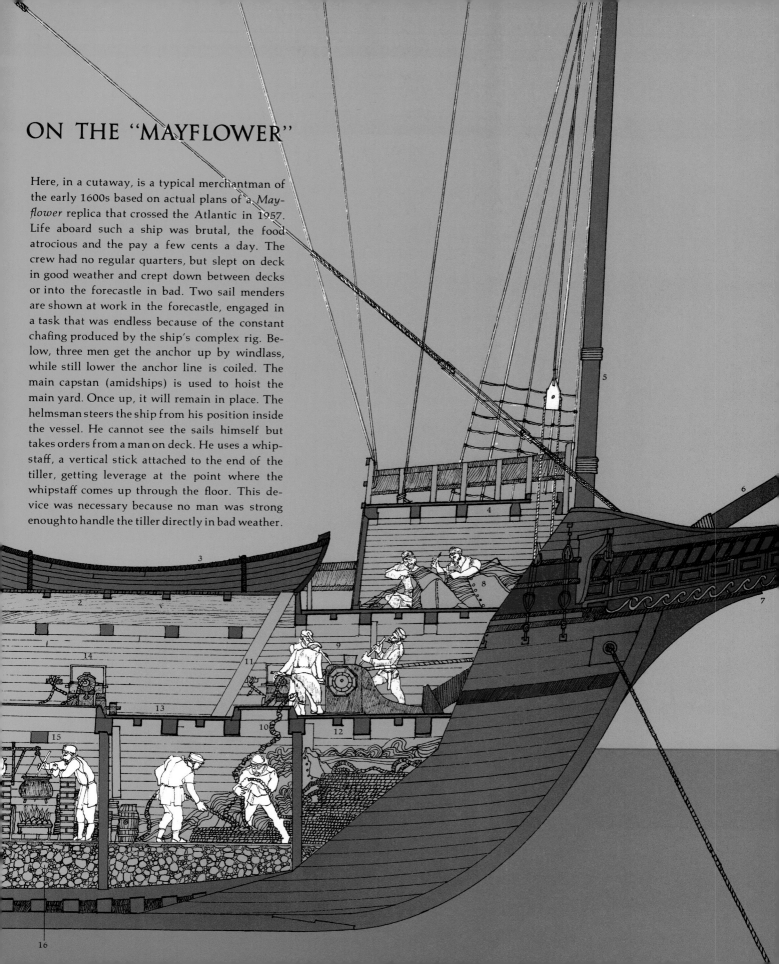

ON THE "MAYFLOWER"

Here, in a cutaway, is a typical merchantman of the early 1600s based on actual plans of a *Mayflower* replica that crossed the Atlantic in 1957. Life aboard such a ship was brutal, the food atrocious and the pay a few cents a day. The crew had no regular quarters, but slept on deck in good weather and crept down between decks or into the forecastle in bad. Two sail menders are shown at work in the forecastle, engaged in a task that was endless because of the constant chafing produced by the ship's complex rig. Below, three men get the anchor up by windlass, while still lower the anchor line is coiled. The main capstan (amidships) is used to hoist the main yard. Once up, it will remain in place. The helmsman steers the ship from his position inside the vessel. He cannot see the sails himself but takes orders from a man on deck. He uses a whipstaff, a vertical stick attached to the end of the tiller, getting leverage at the point where the whipstaff comes up through the floor. This device was necessary because no man was strong enough to handle the tiller directly in bad weather.

Vnt varij dignitatum gradus in China, quorum Man-
dorini sunt præcipui, qui in sellis serico auroque obuelatis
magnifice circumferuntur. Hi sunt qui regnum admi-
nistrant, quorum opera si quis vti velit, atque eo nomi-
ne eos compellare, necesse est, vt procumbens in genua co-
ram illis compareat. Sut proximi à rege, nec præter eos alij per regnũ prin-
cipes habentur, nec ad ea fastigia præter doctos & literatos, vlli euehun-
tur, inter quos quisque eminentior est, prout eruditione fuerit præstan-
tior. Ceteroquin illi ipsi sunt æque gulæ dediti atque vulgus Chinensium,
deliciantur, genioque indulgent terra mariq̃: in quem vsum naues splen-
dide apparatas habent, serico auroque intectas, apposita in medio mensa
opipare instructa.

G   MODVS

5

CATHAY:
THE PERSISTENT VISION

THE MANDARINS OF CHINA, *as depicted in a 16th Century book of travels engraved by Theodor de Bry, enjoyed life when they were not administering or advising the emperor. One (left) is carried about on a stand-up version of a sedan chair, while another entertains aboard his silk-canopied boat.*

The trail-blazing discoveries of Columbus and Da Gama were the starting signals for a succession of 16th Century voyages of exploration to Cathay. Some men headed west, following Columbus, others eastward in the wake of Da Gama, and although both groups found somewhat the same hazards, the eastbound mariners on the whole had an easier time of it.

Renaissance explorers who rounded Africa had maps that clearly indicated the existence of Asia. If the outlines of the Eastern continent—derived from the writings of Ptolemy and Marco Polo—were wildly misleading, they did at least provide a rough guide for voyagers. Moreover, as Da Gama had found, once a traveler reached the east coast of Africa he found himself in the midst of a long-established trading network that extended from the Indian Ocean to India and China. For Europeans, the information provided by local merchants and seamen was invaluable.

The successors to Columbus, on the other hand, faced numerous difficulties. The Americas did not appear on any maps. There were no local pilots, no native charts, no merchant communities familiar with the region. Everything about the new areas—their width, their length, their relationship to Asia—had to be discovered. Considering these handicaps, the speed with which the Americas emerged from the wild conjectures that followed Columbus' landing in the West Indies is much more remarkable than the rapid mapping of the East African coast and the Indian Ocean during the 16th Century.

By 1500, Spanish explorers had mapped the north coast of South America from present-day Maracaibo in Venezuela to Recife on the eastern bulge of Brazil. The next extension of knowledge about the continent possibly took place by accident, and set off a new wave of exploration, this time down the east coast.

During Da Gama's voyage down the west coast of Africa he had encountered savage gales, though he had sailed far out into the Atlantic in an effort to avoid them. Therefore, when Pedro Alvares Cabral of Portugal was sent in 1500 to follow up Da Gama's voyage to India, he was advised to take an even wider detour. Following this advice, Cabral went so far west that he came upon the coast of Brazil, at 17° south. He made no attempt to explore this land, which supports the theory that the discovery was accidental. On the other hand, the King of Portugal had anticipated finding continental land in this part of the earth, which was why he had insisted on moving the Spanish-Portuguese demarcation line established by the pope 270 leagues farther west than Columbus had requested. The fact that Cabral immediately sent one of his ships home with the news argues that he may have been under orders to investigate the existence of a continent; unfortunately his instructions have not survived.

The report Cabral sent to Portugal concluded with a recommendation that a settlement be established in Brazil, for "if there were nothing more than to have here a stopping-place for the voyage to Calicut, that would suffice." Cabral did not know (at any rate he did not say) whether this new land he had found was part of a continent or an island. Columbus had been able to guess from the mighty outflow of the Orinoco that the stretch of Venezuelan coast he visited was part of a great land mass (he still said it was Cathay). Cabral had no such clue, and the answer to the question—island or continent, Cathay or some other place—had to await the cool analysis of another man, the Florentine geographer Amerigo Vespucci.

Vespucci, commanding two privately sponsored Spanish ships, had already seen the north coast of Brazil in the spring of 1499. In 1501, under the Portuguese flag, he again sailed westward, this time to follow up Cabral's discoveries. His journey took him down the east coast from Cape São Roque, near Natal, perhaps as far as the mouth of the River Plate—perhaps even as far as Patagonia; the evidence is unclear.

Vespucci was not a great mariner like Columbus, but he was a man specially trained in the interpretation of discoveries. Unhampered by visions of Cathay or the Terrestrial Paradise, he was more definite than Columbus about the nature of what he had seen, and in 1504 he was quoted as saying that the lands across the ocean comprised a new continent which "it is proper to call a new world." The phrase so greatly excited the German publisher Martin Waldseemüller that he decided to call the new continent by Amerigo Vespucci's name. The world map that Waldseemüller issued in 1507 labeled the southern land "America"—thus doing a grievous and permanent injustice to Columbus. Later, as it became clear that the Americas, north and south, were all one great land mass, Amerigo's name was used not only for the southern part but for the whole.

The realization that this was not Asia but a new continent only spurred the search for an alternate route to the coveted riches of Cathay. Columbus had noticed the strong westward current on the north coast of South America and had reasoned that so huge a volume of water must somewhere find its way into the Indian Ocean. The men who followed him during the early years of the 16th Century accepted Columbus' theory and wasted much time trying to find a sea passage through America to India. But as the true picture of the Caribbean coastline was slowly built up, mariners finally realized that the powerful current had its outlet not to the west but northeastward, in the form of the Gulf Stream. The vision of easy access to Cathay was fading fast.

Meanwhile, European geographers and chartmakers were becoming convinced on their own that Columbus had been wrong and that Asia lay far beyond any of the territories yet explored. How far beyond began to be apparent when, in September 1513, Vasco Nuñez de Balboa, having struggled across the Isthmus of Panama, waded out into the Pacific—in full armor, sword in one hand, the ban-

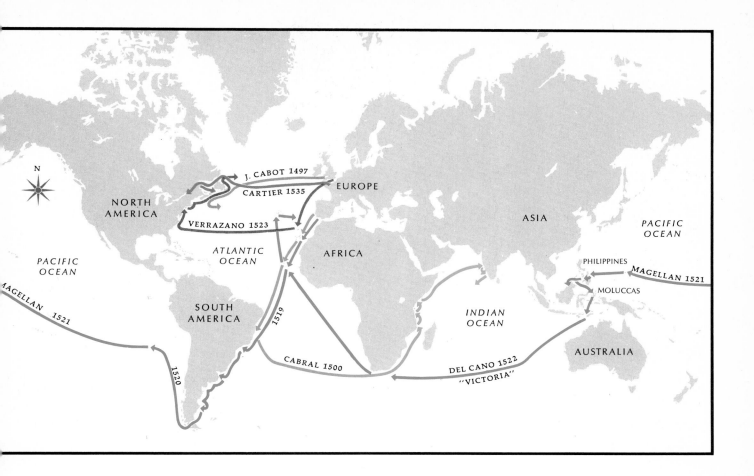

ner of Castile held aloft in the other—to claim the newly discovered ocean for his country. Now it was clear that Asia lay beyond yet another watery horizon.

Spain's hopes of reaching the riches of the Orient, dashed by Balboa, were raised again by a Portuguese aristocrat, Ferdinand Magellan. Magellan had served his country with distinction in the Indies. Then, following a dispute with a superior, he fell into disfavor at the Portuguese court. Unemployed, and seeing no promise of change in the royal attitude, he decided to offer his services to Spain. He was convinced that if Spanish ships could slip under the southernmost point of the American barrier, they would have as easy access to the East Indies as Portugal had found by rounding Africa. During the winter of 1518, he presented this scheme to the Spanish King, Charles I.

Magellan quickly won the King's approval in principle, but he received only halfhearted support when it came to outfitting the expedition. Five aged

ships manned by tatterdemalion crews were all he was given for the long journey. Spain had a good reason for thus limiting its risk: even if Magellan reached the Spice Islands it was by no means certain that Spain could claim them, for no one was sure they lay within the Spanish zone established by the Treaty of Tordesillas.

Leaving Spain in late September, 1519, Magellan nursed his unpromising fleet across the Atlantic to the northeastern coast of Brazil and then turned south to probe for a passage to the Pacific. He followed one false lead up the Bay of Rio de Janeiro, and another up the Estuary of the River Plate. Still he urged his men on until winter set in. Then for the next five months he took refuge in a southern Patagonian bay. During that dreary time of waiting he lost one of his vessels by shipwreck, another by desertion and was almost forced to turn back by a mutiny.

Before sailing on, Magellan captured two Patagonians. He wanted to take them with him, but they were very large and his Spanish sailors were small. "The manner in which he retained them," wrote Antonio Pigafetta, the Italian who was the voyage's chronicler, "was that he gave them many knives, forks, mirrors, bells, and glass, and they held all these things in their hands. Then the captain had some irons brought, such as are put on the feet of malefactors; these giants took pleasure in seeing the irons, but they did not know where to put them, and it grieved them that they could not take them with their hands, because they were hindered by the other things which they held in them." So Magellan obligingly had the shackles put on their legs. It was only when it was too late that "they began to be enraged and to foam like bulls, crying out very loud 'Setebos,' that is to say, the great devil, that he should help them."

At the end of August 1520, Magellan set sail again. It was not until he reached 52° 30′ south that he found the strait that was to bear his name. The passageway was rock-strewn and stormy, but by bullying and cajoling, Magellan got his weary crews through the cliffs and zigzags of the 320-mile-long strait, a masterly piece of seamanship which took him 38 days. When he emerged at Cape Pilar, his theory had been confirmed. There was a southwest passage to the Pacific; America did have a southern tip and did not, as many geographers had believed, form a part of the still unexplored antarctic continent of *Terra Australis Incognita.*

Now Magellan turned north and followed the coast for 1,000 miles, thereby gaining information that would enable chart-makers to gauge the width and shape, as well as much of the extent, of South America. With the easterly trades pushing him on, he turned his leaking ships to the west. Already desperately short of provisions, and with no idea how far he would have to sail before reaching his goal, he forbade his men, under pain of death, to discuss the uncertainties that lay ahead.

By ill luck he followed a course that was nearly all open sea; had he slanted somewhat more to the south he might have come upon idyllic Tahiti, or Samoa or the Fiji Islands. Instead, his men had to endure more than three desperate months of near-starvation and disease. The only group of islands that he encountered was so barren that, breaking his own rule against pessimism, he called them the *Desaventuradas*, the Unfortunate Isles. Not until he reached Guam on March 6, 1521, could he replenish his food supplies. At last, and just in time, it seemed that his luck had changed.

When Magellan arrived at the Philippines on March 16, his spirits soared at the sight of the gold ornaments worn by the natives. Surely Cathay and the wealth he had come to seek were in his grasp. Moving on to investigate the resources of the islands, he landed at Cebu on April 7. There he entered into a treaty of friendship with a native chief. This was to prove disastrous, for in fulfilling his obligations to his new ally, Magellan took part in a skirmish against a rival ruler on the small neighboring island of Mactan—and was killed on April 27. He was thus denied the glory of completing the circumnavigation of the globe, and the certain knowledge that he had succeeded in showing the westward way to the Indies, the task at which Columbus had failed.

For the surviving members of the expedition, the rest of the voyage became a dreary chronicle of misadventure. So few men were left to work the three remaining vessels that one ship was burned and her men were divided between the *Trinidad* and *Victoria.* But the *Trinidad* was in such miserable condition that her captain feared the journey around the Cape of Good Hope; instead he made an unsuccessful attempt to reach Panama, only to be forced back by unfavorable winds. Upon his return to the Moluccas (a part of modern Indonesia) he and his crew were imprisoned by the Portuguese, who had been established there since 1512.

The Magellan expedition's remaining vessel, *Victoria*, piloted by Sebastián del Cano, had meanwhile picked up a good cargo of cloves and other spices in the East Indies, rounded the Cape of Good Hope and limped back to Spain, arriving in Seville on September 8, 1522, to complete the remarkable journey that had begun almost three years before.

Three years later, when four wretched survivors of the *Trinidad* finally got out of Portuguese captivity and made their way home, they increased to 35 the number of men who returned, of the 280 who had set out.

Ironically, the sale of the *Victoria*'s cargo of cloves paid the entire cost of Magellan's expedition, and this indication of the commercial possibilities of the westward route inspired Spain to dispatch two follow-up voyages. Garcia de Loaysa died while leading an expedition in 1525, and only a few wretched survivors reached the Moluccas; in the following year Sebastian Cabot gave up before reaching the Strait of Magellan. It was clear that the rigors of the voyage outweighed its commercial advantages.

Pigafetta's stark narrative of Magellan's voyage is filled with hair-raising tales of rotting stores, splitting sails, starvation and scurvy. The demands made on Magellan's endurance and leadership were so unremitting that it is a wonder the voyage succeeded at all. That it did is a tribute to his ability as a sailor and as a leader. From 1527 on, Spanish attempts to cross the Pacific were made from the halfway house of Mexico.

Magellan had charted South America's west coast as far north as Peru. In the next two decades, Spaniards mapped the remaining gaps in the South American coastline, from Peru to Colombia. Bartolomé Ruiz crossed the equator in his survey of the coasts of Colombia and Ecuador during 1526;

Sebastián de Belalcázar in 1539 and Pedro de Valdivia in 1540 supplied the details of the Peruvian and part of the Chilean shore. All of this knowledge derived from the conquistadors' unceasing search for treasure.

The completion of the North American map took much longer. There was a brief period toward the end of the 15th Century, even before Columbus' voyage, when English sailors made a number of North Atlantic voyages in search of one of the mythical islands, for use as an advanced fishing base. A contemporary English chronicle records, for instance, that "On the 15th of July, 1480, a ship of . . . John Jay, the younger, of 80 ton, sailed from the roadstead of the Port of Bristol . . . with Lloyd, the most scientific mariner in all England, as master; news was received in Bristol on September 18th, that she had sailed the seas for nine [weeks] without finding [an] island, and had been driven by storms into . . . Ireland."

Although voyages such as this failed to locate the sought-after islands, they led to increasing speculation during the 1490s among the Bristol merchants and shipmasters about what actually was to be found across the Atlantic. About 1495, John Cabot arrived in England from Spain with information about Columbus' discoveries, and with a plan to follow his route. Cabot, born Giovanni Caboto in Genoa, was an experienced seaman and his proposal had the full support of Bristol merchants.

King Henry VII authorized the expedition, and in May 1497, Cabot set off in the bark *Matthew* to become the Renaissance discoverer of North America. What part of it he discovered is not certain, for his map and journal are lost. In England it was reported that he had found "two new very large and fertile islands," and that after pursuing a "northerly course . . . at length he fell in with terra firma, where he set up the royal standard."

Another report says that his men "affirm that the sea is covered with fish." The words "islands," "northerly course" and "fish" in these accounts point to a landfall by Cabot in the area of Newfoundland and Nova Scotia.

As optimistic as Columbus, Cabot spread the word that he had reached the fringe of civilized Cathay, with its prized silks. He must have convinced his backers, for he sailed again in 1498, presumably to get nearer to the Cathayan heartland. Of this voyage nothing certain is known. As an aftermath of his failure to find China, Cabot faded into obscurity. Despite his genuine achievement in discovering North America, his name was remembered for long years afterward only because he was the father of another explorer, Sebastian.

During the next 20 years other expeditions were sent to Greenland and Labrador from England and from the Azores, always searching for the elusive Cathay. Little is known about what areas were explored; both England and Portugal finally lost interest when no silk or precious metals were found. Nevertheless, Cabot's discovery of the Grand Banks off Newfoundland, with its immense schools of fish, led to regular and profitable voyages by commercial fishermen.

In retrospect, it is remarkable how the dream of finding Cathay survived repeated disappointments. Even after it had been established that South America was a continent, many Europeans persisted in confusing the geographical relationship of Asia, America and the Pacific Ocean. Balboa's discovery of the Pacific in 1513 and Magellan's voyage six years later were well known and should have dispelled the confusion, but there remained a stubborn hope that Cabot's landfall back in 1497 might indeed have been in the northeasternmost part of China. More than a quarter-century later, still pursuing that dream, Giovanni da Verrazano, a Florentine mariner and surveyor in the service of King

A TALE OF MANY CITIES

When in 1524 Giovanni da Verrazano gazed upon the empty harbor and headlands that would one day be New York, certain other cities destined to share its future were in full maturity, while others were hardly born. The golden domes of Moscow's Archangel Cathedral (above) already glittered over the Kremlin's walls in a city then at the peak of a building boom. Peking, started by the Kublai Khan in the 13th Century, was a walled marvel of pagodas, palaces, terraces and gates.

In Rome, Bramante's magnificent design for St. Peter's was taking shape. In Paris, the Louvre was being turned from a grim old arsenal into a royal palace while a tile works nearby was demolished to make way for the Tuileries. In contrast, Berlin in 1524 consisted of two muddy villages only recently merged to make a capital for gloomy Brandenburg. Tokyo, then called Edo, was little more than a collection of fishermen's huts.

Meanwhile, in the Americas which Verrazano and others were exploring so intently, a far older and more breathtaking city of palaces, pyramids and causeways —the Aztec capital of Tenochtitlán—had just been sacked by a hot-tempered band of Spaniards seeking gold. On the site of its ruins would rise still another New World metropolis: today's Mexico City.

Francis I of France, sailed for North America in 1523.

Verrazano struck the American coast at North Carolina and moved northward. Landing from time to time, but not venturing inland for fear of Indians and animals, "which are much wilder than in our Europe," he compiled from the deck of his ship the first description of the shore and its dwellers from Georgia to Maine. At one point he "discovered a very pleasant spot situated between two hills where a very large river flows into the sea." Lowering a small boat he rowed into New York harbor. "The natives were very much like those we had recently met. . . . They came cheerfully toward us with loud cries of admiration, showing us where we could conveniently ground the boat. We went up river for half a league into the interior and saw that it formed a fine basin about three leagues in circumference."

Verrazano, still expecting to reach Cathay, had not anticipated "such an obstacle of new land, as I found." The fact is that by filling in the gap between Spanish discoveries in the south and English discoveries in the north, his coastal survey had proved that the Americas formed one continuous land mass. Thus his main achievement was to dispel once and for all the notion that America was Asia.

But Verrazano refused to face the facts. Although he had reconciled himself to the reality of continental America, he remained convinced that there must be a gap in the barbarous Atlantic coast which would lead to Asia. When he looked across the Hatteras sandspit off North Carolina and saw the wide waters of Pamlico Sound that lay beyond, he thought he saw not only a strait but the western ocean itself. He promptly concluded that the Pacific invaded the American continent right up to the Carolina cape which juts far out into the Atlantic to constitute one of the worst shipping hazards of that coast. On the map based on his

voyage, and on most of the maps of North America for more than half a century thereafter, the Pacific—under the name "Verrazano's Sea"—is so depicted.

Jacques Cartier, also sailing under the flag of France, was convinced by Verrazano's discoveries that the American continent was not a part of Asia, but he still believed that there must be a passage to the Pacific. He discounted "Verrazano's Sea," and concluded instead that the strait probably existed between Cape Breton and Newfoundland. In 1534 he entered the Gulf of St. Lawrence and found its Labrador coast so bleak that he labeled it "The Land God Gave to Cain." He explored the west coast of Newfoundland and discovered Prince Edward Island, Chaleur Bay and Anticosti Island. Still searching for a strait, he lost much time in a fruitless cruise around Chaleur Bay and then turned back toward France before winter set in. On the way home Cartier gathered from Indians he had taken captive that there was a river—but not a strait—between Anticosti and the Gaspé Peninsula. This was the St. Lawrence, which he had somehow missed in his reconnaissance.

He remembered this during his second expedition in 1535. He had somehow got the impression from the Indians that the river led to native kingdoms as rich as the empires found by Spain in Mexico and Peru. Pursuing this lead, he ascended the St. Lawrence as far as Montreal. There he found an Iroquois village, stoutly palisaded but possessing none of the wealth or culture he had hoped to find. It was late in the year and the Atlantic was 1,000 miles behind him, so he camped for the winter near present-day Quebec. In the fierce weather his men suffered hideously from the cold, from scurvy and from the constant fear of being attacked in their weakened state. In his attempts to find the cause of the disease, Cartier ordered one of the dead men to be dissected. While the post-mortem produced the first clinical description of scurvy, it offered no clue to proper treatment. However, the Indians' remedy, a brew made from hemlock boughs, cured the men who would take it. In the spring, the survivors left for France as soon as the ice on the river melted.

Cartier's tale of hardships was not one to send Frenchmen pouring across the Atlantic. Moreover, King Francis I was too involved with European affairs to give much attention to distant Canada. Cartier made one more voyage in 1541; two years after that, when the Sieur de Roberval returned from an unsuccessful attempt to find the strait to Asia, French interest in North America lapsed, not to revive for 60 years. Nevertheless, the legend of the fabulous kingdoms died slowly. As late as 1634 the Frenchman Jean Nicolet listened to tales of hairless, beardless Indian tribes in the west and went as far as Lake Superior in search of them, convinced that he was about to reach China or Japan.

By comparison with the uncertainties encountered by the explorers who followed Columbus westward across the Atlantic, the chronicle of Portugal's exploitation of Da Gama's route around Africa reads like the sober account of a commercial venture. Portuguese influence in the Indian Ocean was in the nature of an occupation rather than an exploration; their record of the geography of the Indian Ocean was more a translation of local knowledge than an original work of geographical investigation.

This success story begins with Cabral, the man who had inadvertently discovered Brazil. After dispatching a vessel to Portugal with the news of this discovery, he recrossed the Atlantic, got back on course and went on to Calicut. There he established the first Portuguese trading post in India, overriding the hostility and active opposition of the long-established Hindu and Moslem merchant community.

From this slender starting point on the Malabar Coast, Portugal, a nation so far away and so small, created a virtual monopoly of trade in the Arabian Sea. Sailing out of a string of fortified ports in western India, and protected from Arab raiders by ships based at Ormuz and Mombasa, Portuguese vessels regularly carried highly profitable cargoes across to Mozambique and back to Europe around the Cape.

The Portuguese succeeded for a variety of reasons. They skillfully took advantage of the political rivalry that divided the coastal potentates in India; through the vigor of their seamanship they defeated the fleets that tried to break their hold on the carrying trade; their trading posts were protected by brilliantly designed and soundly constructed fortifications, which still stand in Goa and Diu, in East Africa and as far up the Persian Gulf as Bahrein.

In sophisticated territories such as the Malabar Coast, the Portuguese had the advantage of firepower; in less developed lands such as Ceylon, they possessed the additional advantage of surprise. Of the first Portuguese sailors to appear in Ceylon a local chronicler wrote that they were "a race of very white and beautiful people who wear boots and hats of iron and never stop in any place. They eat a sort of white stone [biscuit] and drink blood [wine]. . . . They have guns with a noise like thunder and a ball from one of them, after traversing a league, will break a castle of marble."

The Portuguese swept everything before them, but only in the interest of trade. They stuck to the coasts, content to guard their ports. Not till 1602 did a traveler, the Jesuit Benedict de Goes, leave Agra and strike up north through Lahore into Afghanistan. From there he took the long arc north of the Himalayas to Cathay. The first real survey of

AT THE COURT OF CATHAY, *Marco Polo kneels before the Kublai Khan. Polo's account of his journey in the 13th Century was still, in Columbus' day, the most informative and widely read work on Asia; it influenced almost every later explorer.*

the Indian hinterland had to wait until the beginning of English and French colonial activity in the 18th Century.

Once the Portuguese had clamped on the Indian shore an organization that would secure their trade, they turned their attention still farther east to the richest zones of all. It was during this period that they established trading posts in the Moluccas, sometimes called the Spice Islands. The Portuguese found that their first maps of this area were highly untrustworthy: they either merged all the islands into one huge peninsula east of India, or indicated a random scattering of large islands whose names and positions bore no relation to what actually existed. It was a great stroke of luck, then, when a large chart of the Indian Ocean and Indonesia made by a Javanese pilot fell into Portuguese hands in 1511. The Governor of India, Afonso de Albuquerque, joyously pronounced this "the best thing I have ever seen." Undoubtedly mariners would have

found their own way to the Moluccas, but acquisition of the Javanese chart accounts for the speed with which the East Indies and the South China Sea took shape on Renaissance maps. Malacca was taken over as a fortified base in 1511, in the course of the same expedition that went on to survey Java. By 1526 the immense island of New Guinea had been reached.

Map makers not only secured information from the findings of formal expeditions, but drew on the experience of solitary merchants who moved from harbor to harbor, and of shipwrecked seamen who had seen service under Indonesian chieftains. All of these items, fact and rumor alike, were discussed at Malacca, and pored over and correlated in Lisbon. Cartographically, the result was messy: there was confusion between names; islands which were known only from one landfall were drawn in the wrong scale or amalgamated with other sightings. But slowly the mosaic fell into place. The incitement to further exploration was kept at fever pitch by the variety of native products and luxury goods that awaited a bold mariner, and by the growing rivalry with Spain.

The Treaty of Tordesillas in 1494 had allocated to Portugal all discoveries lying east of longitude 46° 37' west, and gave Spain everything to the west of it. It was only in the following century that the full implications of this barrier began to appear. A meridian of longitude runs clear round the globe, and the location of the Moluccas relative to the line became a matter of intense controversy. It is easy to see today that the demarcation line gave Portugal the Moluccas by a margin of nearly six degrees, but no one could then estimate longitude with accuracy; to ensure their possession against opposing claims by Spain the Portuguese deliberately shifted the position of the islands on the maps they issued.

The result was a furious wrangling between Spain and Portugal, with each side calling in experts who quoted from whatever authority suited their case—Ptolemy and Mandeville as well as the recent voyagers. Then in 1529 the dispute was settled for cash. Charles V, Holy Roman Emperor and King of Spain, was faced with crippling expenditures; to raise money he sold to Portugal for 350,-000 ducats his claim to the Moluccas and the Philippines.

While the exploration of the East Indies was their main preoccupation, the Portuguese also sought trade in the Bay of Bengal on India's east coast, and in Burma, Siam and Cambodia. Consequently, the coastlines of these areas began to appear with some accuracy on maps of the 1530s and '40s.

In 1557 the Portuguese established a still-existing colony at Macao, on the coast of China. However, since China allowed Portuguese merchants to trade only sporadically on the mainland, these en-

ergetic men had also investigated Japan. There they found a kinder, if short-lived, reception—first at Kagoshima, in 1549, then at Nagasaki in 1571. Once these bases had been obtained, and an annual voyage had been organized, starting at Macao with stops at Nagasaki, Malacca and Goa, the exploration of Japan came to a halt, and its geography was not cleared up until the 19th Century. More important to Portugal, and more closely studied, were the Philippines, and in the 1570s Manila emerged as a key port, midway between the silks of China to the north and the spices of the Moluccas to the south.

There was hardly any exploration of mainland China and Southeast Asia in the 16th Century. Although in the West this was precisely the period when one expedition after another was plunging inland into the Americas and replacing myth with fact, the interior of Asia was still thought of in terms of legend. Enough trade could be picked up on the coasts; furthermore, Asia was occupied by governments too efficient to be displaced by the tiny forces Europe was capable of deploying at such long range. Since neither substantial gain nor successful conquest could be achieved by exploration, the hinterlands remained almost untouched. Not until 1598 were the latitudes of China computed; only in 1607 was it definitely confirmed that China was indeed the Cathay that Marco Polo had described so long ago.

For the sake of historical symmetry, the accurate picture of China should have been drawn by professional explorers, thus bringing to a close the work started by their spiritual ancestor, the Portuguese scholar-prince, Henry the Navigator. But in fact this task was accomplished by individual adventurers and missionaries like Benedict de Goes, the man who established the western limits of China and who, dying there at the end of his heroic journey across Turkestan, was accorded this epitaph: "Seeking Cathay he found Heaven."

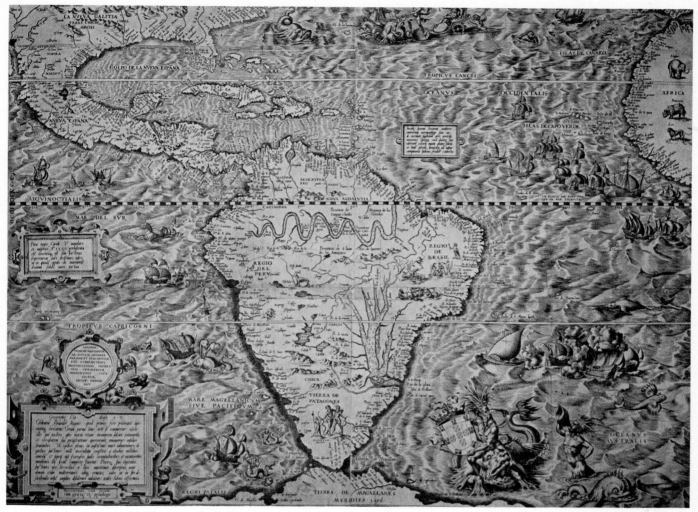

A SNAKELIKE AMAZON, *route of Francisco de Orellana across South America, coils beneath the equator in this map made by Diego Gutiérrez in 1562.*

A STRANGE JUNGLE VOYAGE

"We Spaniards," said the explorer Hernando Cortes, "suffer from a disease that only gold can cure." To seek relief from their malady, and to gain land and glory for themselves and Catholic Spain, the heirs of Columbus turned from their conquest of Mexico and the Caribbean to still greater adventures north and south. Hernando de Soto and Francisco Coronado ranged from Florida to Arizona; Francisco Pizarro conquered the Incas of Peru. Lured on by stories of "El Dorado"—sometimes a golden city, sometimes a chieftain painted with gold dust from head to foot—the tough conquistadors plunged on into the South American interior. Perhaps the most astonishing of these travelers was Francisco de Orellana, a one-eyed knight who in 1541 crossed the Andes to join Pizarro's brother Gonzalo in seeking gold and a "Land of Cinnamon"—and emerged 18 months later at the mouth of the mighty Amazon 3,000 miles away. The country he traversed is much the same today: wild, hostile and in many places still unexplored.

BREACHING THE ANDES

With Orellana not far behind, Gonzalo Pizarro set out from Quito in February of 1541. The first barrier he faced was the great icy wall of the Cordillera de los Andes, whose peaks tower 20,000 feet and more. Up to the cold, windy passes marched his resplendent army of exploration, led by more

than 200 campaign-hardened Spaniards, many in glittering armor, half of them on horse. Four thousand Indians carried supplies and drove herds of pigs along for food; a thousand trained war dogs accompanied them to fight hostile tribes. Then came the first of many adversities that were eventually to reduce Pizarro's proud force to a tattered handful of men. Howling blizzards scattered the soldiers; supplies had to be abandoned; many Indians sickened, deserted or froze to death. As they regrouped and descended into the steaming jungle, the Spaniards found that their adventure had barely begun.

VINE AND LOG BRIDGES, *like this one used by present-day Yagua Indians, were improvised by the Spaniards to get horses and supplies across ravines. The Yaguas seen here still wear fiber headdress and skirts.*

A RUGGED JUNGLE ROAD

Hard on the trail of Pizarro came Orellana and his 23 men, down from the Andes, chopping their way through the stifling rain forest, beating off bands of Indians with horse and lance, crossbow, arquebus and sword. For two months it rained; armor rusted, food spoiled, clothing rotted on their backs.

Finally, in the province of Motín, Orellana caught up with Pizarro. Together they burst out upon a river (the Coca, a high tributary of the Amazon) and slowly worked their way along its banks. But progress was slow and food was desperately scarce. To find the rich lands Indians told them lay downstream, the captains decided to take to the water.

A WATERY HIGHWAY, *this Amazon tributary and others like it were in Orellana's time as today the only practical routes through an otherwise trackless wilderness, where the tangled growth reached up to blot out landmarks, sun and stars.*

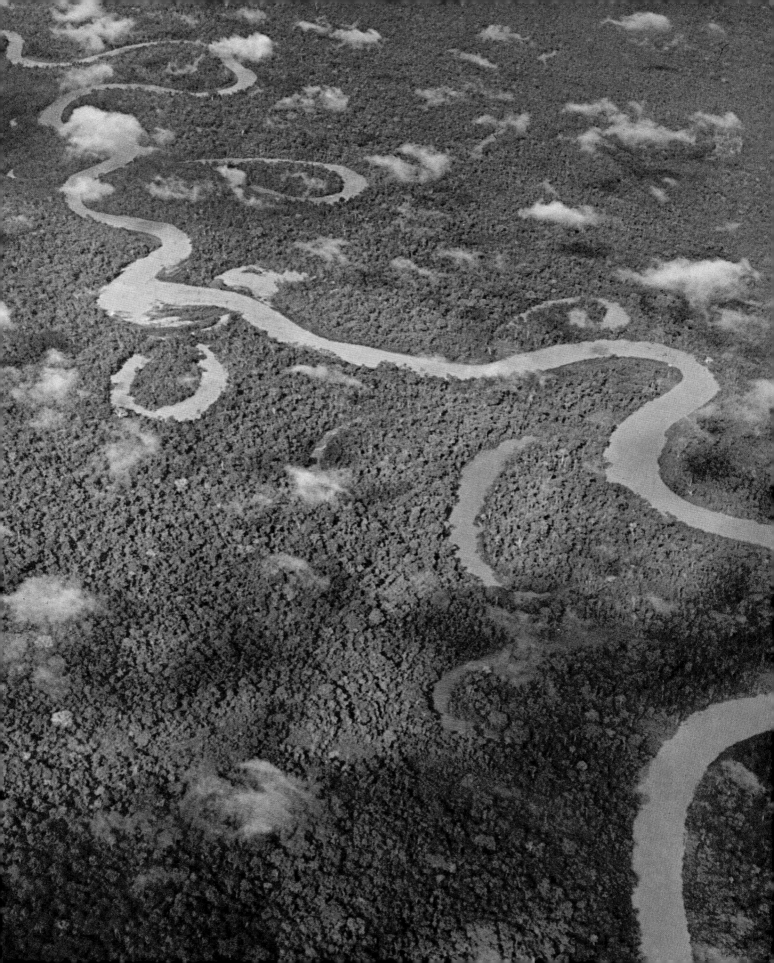

EXOTIC PATTERNS *of fernlike trees mark the jungle's edge, framing the river's broad expanse.* A LONE CANOE, *not unlike some of the warrior dugouts tha*

A HAZARDOUS VOYAGE

On the broad banks of the Coca the Spaniards made camp and set about selecting trees for the ribs and planking of their vessel. Though few were artisans, they managed to make nails from horseshoes, caulking from strips of old shirts and resinous sap, ropes from liana vines. Their "brigantine," *San Pedro*, was little more than an oversized rowboat, but for two months she carried the sick, the priests and the provisions while the main party, on foot, struggled along the riverbank behind.

...arassed Orellana's two small boats, carries an Indian family down more peaceful waters. Even the upper river shown here approaches widths of a half mile.

By now soldiers were dying daily, and Orellana and some 60 men were sent ahead with the boat and several canoes to scout for food. Gonzalo Pizarro never saw him again, though it is not known whether Orellana deserted, was forced by his men to go on, or was prevented by the current from returning. Pizarro, in any case, turned back. Downstream, Orellana's band built a second, stouter boat, the *Victoria*, and continued along the ever-broadening river, stopping at friendly villages,

sacking hostile ones, and fighting violent river storms and occasionally whole fleets of giant war canoes. At one point starvation drove the men to eat their own belts and shoes, boiled in herbs. Toward the end of the voyage Orellana is said to have fought "tall, fair, robust" woman warriors, sent by all-female tribes in the interior. It was after these fierce and quite possibly imaginary ladies, who evoked the Amazons of Greek legend, that the river finally came to be named.

BRILLIANT ORCHIDS *such as the Cattle-ya amethystoglossa were seen by the conquistadors. Like most of the thousands of varieties native to the Amazon, it is an epiphyte, or "air plant," that clings to trees above the ground.*

A GRACEFUL HERON, *one of the countless snowy egrets that dart gently above the river, perches at the water's edge. The voyagers noted that when these birds roosted in flocks, their plumage turned river trees a dazzling white—until, startled, the "blossoms" flew away.*

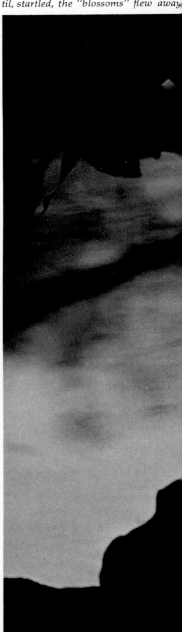

GIANT WATER LILIES, *called Victoria regia, abound in the Amazon's quieter waters. During floods the Spaniards saw whole islands of vegetation floating past them, uprooted from the river's banks.*

THE AMAZON'S UNEXPECTED TREASURE

Although Indians kept telling them of rich kingdoms always farther on, Orellana's men never saw more gold than a few trinkets. The treasure they did find was the broad highway of the river itself, and a thousand sights along it that matched its own fierce beauty. Beneath the high green canopies of jungle the travelers glimpsed wild orchids, long-tailed parrots, blue butterflies and forest moths with wings nearly a foot across. Crossbowmen and net tenders were kept busy supplying the hungry men with iguana, spider monkeys, giant turtles and fish. But if some days seemed paradise, the jungle nights were more like hell: everywhere there were jaguar, crocodiles, anacondas, inch-long biting ants, and piranha—fish which could strip a man to a skeleton in minutes if he fell overboard.

OUT OF THE RIVER'S MOUTH —A JOURNEY'S END

As the two tiny boats drifted on, it seemed they were no longer on a river, but in a maze of islands on a great, moving inland sea. On one of these islands they beached their hand-made river craft and refitted for the sea voyage ahead, adding decking, new masts and blankets sewn together for sails.

Setting out through the Amazon's main delta, which is 150 miles across, the 45 remaining men struggled northward to reach the Spanish island of Cubagua off the Venezuelan coast. Some 17 months after parting with Pizarro, Orellana arrived in Spain to convince his king that he was not a deserter, but the discoverer of a vast new territory for the Crown. Later he returned to his land of Amazons with a governor's appointment and 400 men. But this time the river's size and savagery defeated him. His men sickened and scattered, and Orellana himself died while exploring the river's mouth.

6

NORTH
TO THE ORIENT

In 1527, summing up the results of the preceding century of exploration, the English merchant Robert Thorne wrote: "There is one way [left] to discover, which is into the North. For out of Spain they have discovered all the Indies and seas occidental, and out of Portugal all the Indies and seas oriental." These words afford a key to a century of heartbreaking efforts by the nations of northern Europe, notably England and Holland, to catch up with Portugal and Spain by finding polar routes to the Indies.

Except for a few shadowy voyages by John Cabot and others toward the end of the 15th Century, English interest in exploration had been slow to develop. Lacking the surplus manpower that enabled Spain to recruit adventuresome young men, untouched by the crusading zeal that stirred Portugal, England had concentrated on domestic affairs while the Iberian nations opened sea routes to the far corners of the world.

By the 1540s, however, Turkish pirates had made the Mediterranean increasingly dangerous and had discouraged English ships from picking up spices at Levantine ports. At about the same time, Spain and Portugal increased their control over lanes to the Indies. English merchants, blocked from their supplies toward the south, took an increasing interest in the possibilities of the north.

What little was known about conditions in the north should have discouraged all thought of subpolar expeditions. All the normal hazards of exploration were present in these northern voyages with the exception of thirst: ice and snow could save life as well as take it. Storms were as brutal as in the tropics, scurvy as fatal. No seaman would face a tiger or be charged by an elephant, but many would fall victim to polar bears, as on Willem Barents' expedition in 1595. The Eskimos could be unpredictably savage or clownish—descriptions of fur-clad hunters dancing clumsily to Elizabethan music, or exchanging animal noises with their English visitors, are amusing; they could, on occasion, be hostile.

The tropics could be navigated all the year round, but the blizzards of the Arctic winter acted as a blindfold for months on end. Ice packs caught and crushed ship after ship. Compass variation in the

ICEBOUND OFF SIBERIA *while seeking a northeast route to China in 1596, crewmen from the ship of Dutch explorer Willem Barents shoot a polar bear for food. Their craft was thrust upward and slowly crushed by the ice. The crew wintered on a nearby island in a hut built from their ship's hull.*

far north was wilder, and the rapidly dwindling length of a degree of longitude made it almost impossible to calculate an exact position or to record the Arctic jigsaw of straits, fiords and islands. So it was more difficult for successive voyagers to learn from those who had gone before.

Cartography was further complicated by the fact that medieval map makers had endowed the northern seas, like the southern, with mythological islands. The most important of these was said to be Frisland, which seems to have been born out of confusion between an imaginary island and the actual southern part of Greenland. Well into the 18th Century, explorers' maps clearly depicted Frisland, separating it from the northern part of Greenland by a wide and, of course, nonexistent strait.

No matter how terrible the difficulties encountered, the search for a northern passage persisted. This stubbornness sprang in part from the magnitude of the prize which success would bring. If Cathay could be reached from the north, then the wharves of Bristol and London and Amsterdam would groan under the weight of the same precious cloves and peppers, cinnamon and nutmegs that perfumed the warehouses of Lisbon and Seville.

Although the profit motive was a powerful spur to England's northern expeditions that began in the mid-16th Century, the desire for wealth was mingled with sheer intellectual curiosity. English merchants seeking to preserve their share of the spice trade obtained some support from Tudor and Stuart monarchs, but never as much as the rulers of Spain and Portugal gave to their explorers and traders. The deficit was made up through the investments of private enthusiasts eager to understand the geography of the far north and fertile with ideas for the solution of the navigational problems that would be met in subpolar waters.

The enthusiasts were a strangely mixed group. Some were stay-at-home intellectuals like the brilliant mathematician John Dee, who was suspected of dealing in black magic; some were scholarly seamen like John Davis and Sebastian Cabot; some were gentry, like Sir Humphrey Gilbert, who were not only brave and idealistic enough to take risks, but scholars enough to have studied which risks had a fair chance of success.

The most significant impetus to the northern voyages came from a group of merchants of a type new in England. These men took pride in their money-making careers. But they were not only determined to take advantage of England's new social mobility, which enabled a prosperous merchant to become absorbed into the gentry; they were touched more directly than any other English social group by the educational fervor of the Renaissance. Sober, intelligent and patriotic, such men found it easy to understand the scholars of exploration and to enlist the sympathetic support of solid gentlemen who had the ear of the Crown.

Once the English made up their minds to reach Cathay from the north, they had to decide whether to make the attempt via the northeast or the northwest. They never quite came to a final decision; now the northeast was favored, now the northwest. The chronicle of northern expedition has a zigzag, not a straight-line, character.

Two reasons—one geographic, the other economic—lay behind the initial concentration on finding a northeast passage. Relying on the writings of medieval Arab geographers, John Dee and other theorists of the 16th Century argued that after passing Cape Tabin (a mythical headland whose position roughly corresponded to the present-day Taymyr Peninsula in north-central Siberia), the explorer would find that the north coast of Asia trended southeast into more temperate waters.

This promise of an easy voyage was buttressed by the prospect of the financial advantages that England might expect from the northeast route.

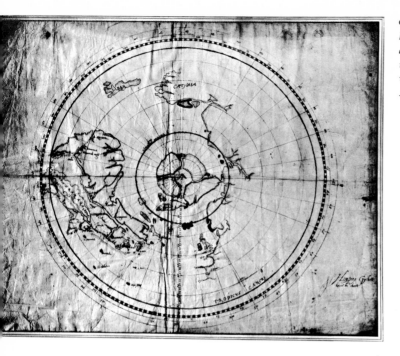

CLEAR SAILING TO CATHAY *is shown on this English map, drawn on a polar projection about 1582. Cartographers wrongly thought the North Pole was surrounded by navigable waters that included a sea lane above North America (left) leading to the Pacific (top).*

England's main industry was the production of heavy cloth. While it was suspected that the people who lived near the northwest passage around North America were unsophisticated savages, content with skins and furs, the people of northern Asia were seen as part of the civilization of Cathay, willing to exchange silks and other southern luxuries for the warm and durable English cloth. There was thus an extra advantage to the northeast passage. If the final approaches to Cathay should be blocked for some reason, then all would not have been in vain, for a profitable trade could still be carried on with those who lived along the earlier stages of the route.

Accordingly, in 1553, Sir Hugh Willoughby left with three ships bound for Cathay. His fleet was scattered by storms but he held his own vessel on course past Norway's North Cape until he discovered the southwest coast of the Novaya Zemlya archipelago. By this time summer was fading, so he withdrew to winter in Lapland. Ignorant of the advantages of ice igloos, the crew remained on board ship. When spring came Willoughby and all his men were dead from the cold, or scurvy, or both. Meanwhile, aboard another vessel, Willoughby's second-in-command, Richard Chancellor, had pene-

trated the White Sea to Archangel. From there he traveled overland to Moscow. The search for the passage had failed, but an important trading link with Russia had been forged, and this promised still richer contacts beyond Novaya Zemlya.

The next reconnaissance was carried out in 1556 by Stephen Burrough. This remarkable voyage was executed in a single tiny vessel, the *Searchthrift*, with a total crew of eight. In a touching passage Burrough describes his departure. Sebastian Cabot, by then in his eighties and the Grand Old Man of English pilotage, came down to Gravesend in person to wish Burrough Godspeed. Cabot was "accompanied with divers gentlemen and gentlewomen who, after that they had viewed our pinnace and tasted of such cheer as we could make them aboard, they went on shore, giving to our mariners right liberal rewards. . . . And then at the sign of the Christopher [Inn] he and his friends banquetted and made me and them that were in the company great cheer. And for very joy that he had to see the towardness of intended discovery, he entered into the dance himself amongst the rest of the young and lusty company, which being ended, he and his friends departed most gently, commending us to the governance of almighty God." Ahead lay freezing gales and months in the unknown, but Burrough and his crew would always remember the gay farewell party.

The little boat survived constant perils from storm, fog and ice as it moved through the icy seas toward Novaya Zemlya. Once a whale as large as the *Searchthrift* itself surfaced alongside. Burrough discovered Vaigach Island, set like a stepping stone between Novaya Zemlya and the mainland. Passing the island, he found the ice-blocked entrance to the Kara Sea.

There he made contact with the Samoyeds, nomadic tribesmen who were, alas, very un-Cathayan. Their idols, Burrough wrote, were "the worst . . .

that ever I saw. The eyes and mouths of sundry of them were bloody. They had the shape of men, women and children very grossly wrought, and that which they had made for other parts was also sprinkled with blood." One of Burrough's men, Richard Johnson, later described one priest's grotesque rite. The Samoyed heated a sword in the fire "and thrust it through his body, as I thought, in at his navel and out at his fundament; the point being out of his shirt behind I laid my finger on it. Then he pulled out the sword and sat down."

Like Willoughby, Burrough was forced to retreat from the closing ice. He wintered successfully in the White Sea near Archangel, and in the spring he returned home.

For a while the merchants who had financed these northeasterly voyages paused, content with the successful Russian trade via the White Sea. Moreover, the debate between the proponents of the northeast and northwest passages was becoming more heated, and prudence suggested a halt until the dispute was resolved.

Sir Humphrey Gilbert, half-brother of Sir Walter Raleigh, was the most eloquent advocate of the northwest route. An excellent representative of the almost uniquely English class of men who combined daredeviltry, a sound education and native shrewdness, Gilbert made an elaborate case to counter the northeasterners' brief. His principal antagonist was Anthony Jenkinson, who had sailed to Russia and crossed that country down to the Caspian Sea. Some time in the winter of 1565-1566, Gilbert and Jenkinson argued the whole question of polar routes before Queen Elizabeth.

Jenkinson's arguments survive only in Gilbert's references to them, as set forth in an account that he wrote of his own case which he published 10 years later as the *Discourse of a Discovery for a New Passage to Cathay*. A glance at this record will show the atmosphere, half credulous, half

shrewd, in which the northward projects were born.

Gilbert's general thesis, which was fairly widely accepted by geographers, conceded that a northeast passage existed, but asserted that it was far more difficult than the northwest passage and involved going much farther north. On the northwest route, Gilbert continued, once Labrador was rounded, the coast trended steadily southward through a passage called the Strait of Anian into the Pacific. In modern terms, Gilbert's north coast would run from Hudson Strait to Seattle, so most of the voyage would be in seas where the temperature resembled that of England.

It is revealing to watch how Gilbert attacks Jenkinson point by point, and develops his own argument. As no man had traveled either route, each of the debaters had to rely on available information about the approaches to the northern passages, and most of this was hearsay evidence, either from contemporaries or ancient writers.

Jenkinson, however, had actually spoken to a Tartar fisherman who said that he had followed the northeast passage a long way and still saw clear sea far ahead of him. "Whereunto I answered," wrote Gilbert, "that the Tartarians were a barbarous people, and utterly ignorant in the art of navigation. . . . Further, no-one can see more than 20 miles ahead at sea." Jenkinson next produced the fact that a unicorn's horn had been found on the coast of Barents Sea; since those magical beasts were known to flourish in Cathay, the horn must have arrived at its destination by floating along the northeast passage. To this Gilbert retorted that the horn would have sunk long before it reached Europe. And why look to Asia for the source of the horn, asked Gilbert, when eminent medieval authorities confirmed that Scandinavia was the home of a one-horned beast called Asinus Indicus, not to mention a fish with a long horn? (The beast, of course, was mythical; the "fish" was the narwhal,

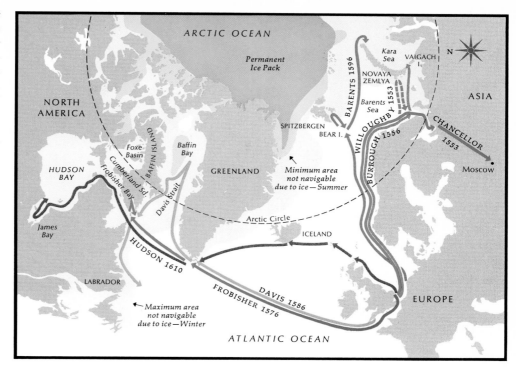

NORTHERN PASSAGES *to Asia were sought by scores of explorers, some of whose routes are shown here. Willoughby and Chancellor and Burrough and Barents tried the northeast but were blocked by Russia. A northwest passage was the goal of the Englishmen Frobisher, Davis and Hudson, but instead they discovered areas in the upper reaches of North America. The extent of navigable waters around the North Pole's permanent ice pack (dark blue) is shown at its maximum (light blue) and minimum (medium blue).*

probably the source of all "unicorn" horns, but Gilbert's explanation was a lucky guess.)

Having refuted Jenkinson's argument to his own satisfaction, Gilbert now took the offensive. He quoted Pliny to the effect that "there were certain Indians driven by tempest upon the coast of Germany." Other Indians had arrived on the same shore, Gilbert added, as recently as 1160. Gilbert was certain that these visitors had come from Cathay via the northwest passage, and he gave his reasons. Contrary winds and high seas ruled out the route around the Cape of Good Hope for the small boats used by the Indians. Had the Indians come overland from Asia, there would have been reports extant of their journey through southern Europe.

As for the northeast passage, Gilbert dismissed it by pointing to the discouraging experience of English seamen who had tried to break past Novaya Zemlya into the Kara Sea. How could the voyagers from Cathay have sailed through the hostile Arctic? It is well known, said Gilbert, that "the piercing cold of the gross thick air so near the Pole will so stiffen and fur the sails and ship tackling that no mariner can either hoist or strike them. Also, the air is so darkened with continual mists and fogs so

near the Pole that no man can well see either to guide his ship or direct his course. Also the compass at such elevation doth very suddenly varie; which things must of force have been their destructions, although they had been men of much more skill than the Indians are."

Gilbert concluded that all of his evidence made up a watertight case for the northwest passage as the only feasible northern route to Cathay. There was a passage, and England must take advantage of it. Columbus had discovered America with much less evidence to go on. England must catch up. The northwest passage was shorter than the Spanish or Portuguese routes, and freight charges on the produce of Cathay would be accordingly less.

There was another advantage, said Gilbert: "we might inhabit some part of those countries and settle there such needy people of our country which now trouble the commonwealth, and through want here at home are enforced to commit outrageous offences, whereby they are daily consumed with the gallows." These "needy people" would form a settlement which could act as a staging post—the Mozambique of North America—for vessels plying the northwest passage, and also act as a center for the trade in furs and dried fish. Thus, almost as an afterthought, Gilbert advanced the only one of his ideas that was to prove significant—English colonization of North America.

Quite apart from Gilbert's passionate advocacy, the prospects for success in the northwest seemed good. Men remembered that as early as 1509 Sebastian Cabot had seen the entrance to a large inlet, the present-day Hudson Bay. Although Cabot had turned back, blocked by ice floes and the refusal of his mutinous crew to go farther, the bay just might have marked the predicted southward turning of the coast toward the Strait of Anian. Better still, the bay might itself be a linking strait to the Pacific. Other men pointed to "Verrazano's Sea" near North Carolina as an indication of how close the Pacific might be. Actually, few hardheaded geographers really believed that a strait would be found much below the latitude of northern Labrador; it was, however, almost an article of faith that the strait, when found, would trend sharply to the southwest and bring ships swiftly to the Pacific.

It took more than a decade for the arguments of Gilbert and Dee to win support for an expedition to the northwest. When the money was raised, it came largely from Michael Lok, a merchant who was attracted both by the fascinating geographical theory and the prospect of substantial profits. Stephen Burrough was called in to add his knowledge of the conditions to be met in Arctic waters. And Martin Frobisher was named commander of the expedition.

An experienced and fearless captain, Frobisher had learned his trade during voyages to the Guinea coast of Africa, and had sharpened his seamanship as a pirate preying on Spanish ships in the English Channel. For the journey to the north, he was provided with two small vessels, the *Gabriel* and the *Michael*, and a little pinnace. In June 1576, Queen Elizabeth granted him a farewell audience, after which he set sail, his spirits buoyed by the opti-

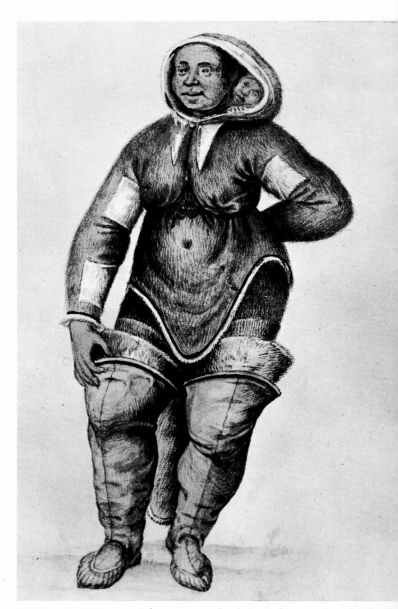

DRESSED IN SEALSKINS, *an Eskimo woman—her baby peeking out from her hood- is seen in a painting by the 16th Century English artist John White. White proba- bly accompanied Martin Frobisher on his second voyage to the northwest, where Frobisher saw the mother and child on Baffin Island in 1577 and took them aboard*

mistic forecasts of some of England's best brains.

By the time he passed to the south of Greenland, Frobisher had lost his pinnace in a storm, and the *Michael* had deserted. Nevertheless he took the *Gabriel* beyond Resolution Island at the entrance to Hudson Strait and found what he thought was the opening of the promised route to the Strait of Anian and Cathay. It was, in fact, a bay, but he was not able to get far enough to realize this. Sailing westward he gleefully named the "channel" Frobisher's Strait (today, Frobisher Bay) and landed to make contact with a party of Eskimos. But the Eskimos were in no mood for friendship; they captured five Englishmen and their longboat, leaving Frobisher with only 13 men. Perhaps in anger, perhaps to vent his frustration, Frobisher, an immensely powerful man, leaned over the rail and lifted another Eskimo, kayak and all, out of the water and onto the *Gabriel*'s deck as a souvenir. Then he turned for home.

The souvenir was a great success. For, as Christopher Hall, the *Gabriel*'s pilot wrote, the Eskimos "be like to Tartars, with long black hair, broad faces and flat noses." Since Tartaria was in Asia, it seemed plausible that the new strait did indeed divide America from Asia and lead to Cathay. But Frobisher had brought another souvenir as well: samples of black stone which appeared to contain streaks of gold.

His gold was no more real than his strait, but it gained him backers for two further expeditions, both fruitless, in 1577 and 1578. During the third voyage, Frobisher lost a ship to wind and ice. One of his companions recalled the incident in a description that could be applied to almost every Arctic voyage: "The storm still increased and the ice enclosed us, so that we were fain to take down . . . top masts. For the ice had so environed us that we could see neither land or sea as we could ken, so that we were fain to cut our cables to hang overboard for fenders, somewhat to ease the ship's sides from the great and dire strokes of the ice; some

with capstan bars, some fending off with oars, some with planks of two inches thick which were broken immediately with the force of the ice; some going out upon the ice to bear it off with their shoulders from the ships."

On his last two trips, Frobisher was more interested in finding gold than in exploring for a passage. But he made one observation that was to haunt future expeditions. As he sailed amid the confusing welter of islands and ice, he decided that the great bay, first seen by Sebastian Cabot nearly 70 years before, was likely to be the promised passage. This conclusion was the bane of many of the subsequent explorers in this area; Hudson Bay became as baffling a puzzle to seekers of the northwest passage as the Kara Sea was for searchers in the northeast.

Frobisher's successive failures contributed to the bankruptcy of his patrons and to a marked lessening of enthusiasm for further exploration of the northwest. Once again English interest in the search for a northeast route revived, this time because Turkish aggression in Persia had cut off the rich flow of eastern products up the Volga to Archangel and thence to England. So in 1580 another northwest passage expedition was fitted out.

By the standards of that day, the planning was excellent. Stephen Burrough was called in again to give practical advice. John Dee, willing to argue for any route as long as it was to the north, provided theoretical encouragement by assuring those concerned that no part of the north Asian coast was nearer the Pole than Norway's North Cape. Since Willoughby and Burrough had already successfully passed North Cape at 71° north, Dee's pronouncement augured well for success. In fact the Taymyr Peninsula—which would have to be rounded—reaches almost to 78°, the fringe of the permanent icecap, an impossible barrier for the stoutest sailing vessel. But Dee could point to support from the greatest European authority of all, Gerhardus Mercator, who had written to Richard Hakluyt to say that "the voyage to Cathay by the east is doubtless very easy and short, and I have oftentimes marvelled that being so happily begun it hath been left off."

Two vessels were sent, commanded by Arthur Pet and Charles Jackman. According to their precise instructions, the two captains were to sail by Burrough's chart until they were past the Kara Sea. They were then to double the mythical Cape Tabin, making charts as they went; it would take them less than a month, said Dee confidently. After passing the cape, they could either go straight to the capital of Cathay via "the famous river Oechardes" (an echo of some medieval knowledge of the River Lena in eastern Siberia) or, if they preferred, they could sail on southeastward until they came to the great port of Quinsay in northern China. They might then proceed to Japan, and they should in any case keep their ears open for news of Francis Drake, who was believed to be pushing across the Pacific at the moment. If they found him, they were to lead him home through the northeast passage and save him the trouble of returning via the Indian Ocean.

On May 30, Jackman in the *William* and Pet in the *George* left Harwich. In August they were still contending desperately with ice in the Kara Sea, fending it off, losing sight of each other amid it, mooring themselves to a piece of it to catch their breath, then hurriedly casting off to avoid being rammed by another iceberg. They groped their way, haunted by this silent army of white shapes whose ranks opened and closed confusingly about them. At last they turned back in exhaustion. Pet battled storms and reached home with his crew almost dead from exposure. Jackman, on the *William*, perished with all hands off the coast of Norway.

With this repulse, English interest in the northeast was finished for good. The stage was taken again by the undiscouraged protagonists of the northwest passage, with a new cast that included

gentry like Sir Walter Raleigh and Sir Francis Walsingham, and wealthy merchants like William Sanderson. To follow the trail so tantalizingly blazed by Frobisher, these sponsors nominated John Davis, a remarkably able sailor.

Davis was a very different sort from his predecessor. Frobisher had the courage and the authority needed for exploration, but he lacked the science; as a discoverer he was diverted by the freebooter's eye for treasure. Davis was a dogged and scholarly navigator, undeflected by personal ambition, undeterred by disappointments. His first voyage, in 1585, was cut short by storms, but he went farther north than Frobisher and discovered Cumberland Sound before the winter ice forced him to return. A second voyage, the following year, added little. His third and last journey, in 1587, took him high up the west coast of Greenland into Baffin Bay, but a huge ice pack forced him to turn back at the highest latitude yet reached in these voyages. He was still optimistic. "I have been in seventy-three degrees," he wrote to one of his backers, "finding the sea all open, and forty leagues between land and sea. The passage is most probable, the execution easy. . . ."

Davis repeated his belief that "there is a short and speedie passage into the South Seas . . . by northerly navigation" in a work he called *The Worldes Hydrographical Description*, but by the time money and support became available for another expedition he was dead.

Despite Davis' assurances, it seems almost unbelievable that other expeditions should have followed on the heels of all these failures. Yet intelligent men continued to search for the passage around North America. One of the best known was Henry Hudson, who had previously sailed to Novaya Zemlya for the English, and had explored Delaware Bay and the Hudson River as far as Albany for the Dutch.

English backers sent Hudson off again, in 1610. He led a modest expedition consisting of only one

ship, *The Discovery*. After passing through Hudson Strait, he saw a vast expanse of water extending south and west before him. The Pacific, he concluded, was within his reach. But as he headed south into Hudson Bay, he was increasingly puzzled by the thickening ice. Finally, disillusioned, he reached a dead end at James Bay. There he had to winter. It was a ghastly experience for the crew, made all the more difficult by Hudson's inability to get on well with his men. When spring freed his ship from the ice, he announced his intention of searching farther for a passage. But his crew mutinied. The sailors forced Hudson, his son and five loyal sailors into an open boat, towed it through the ice floes and cut it adrift. They were never seen again.

Back in England, the mutineers' guilt was evident.

But they were too valuable to hang, for they alone could retrace the path to the promised passage. Hudson's voyage had proved that it did not proceed from the southern end of Hudson Bay, so it must lie westward across the huge inlet. With great enthusiasm a Northwest Company was formed, supported by nearly 300 investors, from the Archbishop of Canterbury down to three of the mutineers themselves. With the incredible stubbornness that marked all of the northern ventures a series of expeditions set out and explored Hudson Bay with no success; then, for 15 years other, more northerly routes were tried; finally, in 1631, Luke Foxe and Thomas James made the last attempts of that era to find the northwest passage.

None of these could succeed. There was in fact a

northwest passage through Foxe Basin into the Gulf of Boothia and then west through Lancaster Sound, but it was not suited to sailing vessels, and, choked with ice almost all the year round, it was hard to recognize as a passage at all. William Baffin indeed found the entrance to Lancaster Sound in 1616, but saw nothing but ice as solid as the land. Much was learned: northern Labrador, a good deal of Baffin Island and the islands to the north of Hudson Bay were charted. And much was suffered: the exploration of no other area claimed so many lives.

Although the English had given up, others attempted the northeast route. At the end of the 16th Century, for instance, Willem Barents, a great Dutch navigator, made three unsuccessful attempts to get beyond the Kara Sea. On the last of these expeditions in 1596, Barents went far to the north and discovered Spitsbergen. Turning east, he was trapped by the ice and forced to winter in a bay on the east coast of Novaya Zemlya.

Barents' crew was lucky enough to find driftwood with which to build a house, guarded by a snowman in the form of a polar bear which they killed, allowed to freeze and set up on its stiffened feet. There they passed the winter, with the snow rising past the door and scurvy striking one after the other, and with their ship forced ever higher from the sea by the pressure of the ice. When spring came it was clear that there was no chance of freeing their vessel, so they set out for home in two open boats. Barents and one of his crew, weakened by disease, died off the coast of Novaya Zemlya, but the others were picked up by Russian vessels and eventually reached Holland. Nearly three centuries later a Norwegian seal hunter, Captain Elling Carlsen, visited Ice Haven, where the Dutch had wintered and found their house. Among its pitiful relics was a note written by Barents to the effect that he had been held up by ice en route to Cathay.

In some ways the search for northeast and northwest passages is the most bizarre episode in the history of exploration. A glance at a map showing the seasonal limits of pack ice will explain why it was not until 1878-1879 that a Swedish vessel, Baron Nils Nordenskiöld's *Vega*, sailed around northern Europe and Asia. The more tortuous northwest passage was not threaded until 1906, when Roald Amundsen accomplished the feat after a three-year voyage, remaining immobilized in the ice during the worst weather.

Knowing what Renaissance explorers did not— that their efforts were doomed in advance—it is a harrowing experience for the modern reader to watch these valiant men search for a gap in the impenetrable wall of ice. In their indomitable efforts, the captains and crews of these expeditions have a fascination akin to that possessed by the tragic heroes of classical drama as they struggle to escape the iron embrace of destiny.

If the explorers themselves brought back nothing more valuable than a few skins and walrus tusks, they were followed by hundreds of vessels that made regular annual voyages as far as Baffin Bay and Spitsbergen for cod and whale and seal. This steady traffic, which made the hazardous seem humdrum, helped to bridge the periods of disillusion between the failure of one series of expeditions and the fitting out of the next.

For Renaissance explorers the polar routes were an irresistible fantasy. They were not routes to Cathay. They are only practicable for vessels constructed to smash ice or to go under it, like the nuclear submarine *Nautilus*, which surfaced near the Pole in 1958. For this reason, the men who struggled and died in the Arctic cannot be said to have advanced the course of civilization by much. Nevertheless, the succession of seamen who sailed into those icy culs-de-sac deserve to be ranked among the supreme exemplars of the remarkable questing spirit of the Age of Exploration.

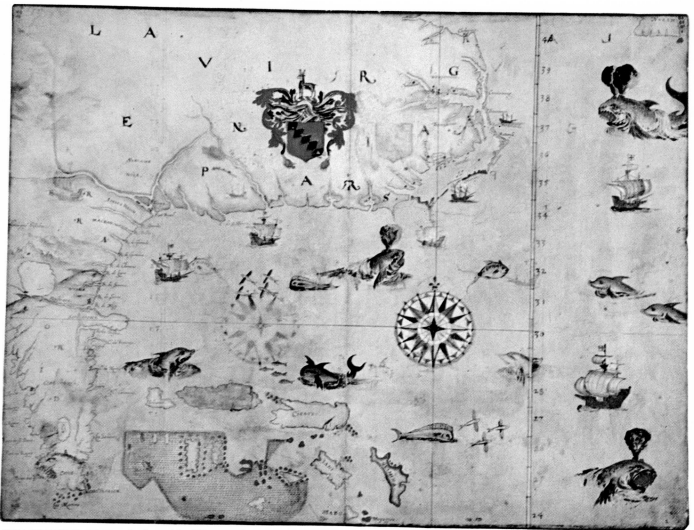

THE LAND CALLED VIRGINIA *is charted by White, with the seal of Raleigh prominently on view. Exaggerated New World sea creatures swim offshore.*

THE FIRST AMERICANS

Long after the early explorers established the existence of the New World, it remained a land of fantasy to most Europeans. It was not until 1585 that an artist, John White, landed at Roanoke Island off North Carolina under assignment from Sir Walter Raleigh to paint truthfully the men, flora and fauna of the New World. Copies of his work, published later, created tremendous interest as Europeans took their first real look at the inhabitants of the new land. In all, White made three trips to North America, one as governor of the famous Lost Colony of Roanoke Island. In later centuries his art fell into obscurity. Today, however, his works are recognized as masterpieces of their kind—remembrances of the days when the English and the original Americans first met face to face.

THE PROTECTED VILLAGE LIFE

When the Indians of Roanoke Island saw the first English ship sailing into their harbor they fled in panic. But gradually the English gained their confidence by offering glass beads and dolls as signs of friendship. As the explorers observed Indian life they grew more and more astonished. Though "savages," the Indians were gentle in demeanor, and their relationships with one another were built on mutual concern. They lived by hunting and fishing, and resided in tiny villages, the largest of which had only 30 shelters.

Yet, although Indian community life was harmonious, the tribes were subject to sudden black moods; at such times they were likely to launch sneak attacks on their neighbors. For this reason many of the villages were walled with pointed wooden stakes.

INDIANS—*a squaw and baby at left, a warrior at right—are portrayed by White. White proved himself a good observer but no master artist: his Indians resemble muscular Englishmen carrying bows and arrows.*

E INDIAN VILLAGE *of Pomeiock (above)*
1 18 shelters protected by a fence
:h a narrow entrance. The shelters
re draped with grass matting, which
ld be rolled up to let in light and air.

CAMPFIRE SONGS, *offering thanks for protection from the perils of daily life, are sung by a group of men and women. They accompany themselves with rattles made of gourds filled with fruit pits.*

THE ABUNDANT WATERS OF THE NEW WORLD

White's assignment was to paint the New World in glowing colors, so English settlers would be attracted there. It was an easy job. The land and waters offered food in abundance. In particular, the visiting Englishmen saw and tasted a succulent variety of fish, shellfish, oysters and tortoises.

The Indians harvested the waters in remarkable ways. According to Thomas Hariot, a settler who later published a report in England, the Indians used long, sharpened poles which they tossed at the fish "much as Irishmen cast darts." They also trapped fish in ingenious reed weirs. "It is a pleasing picture," Hariot wrote, "to see these people wading and sailing . . . sharing all those things with which God has so bountifully provided them."

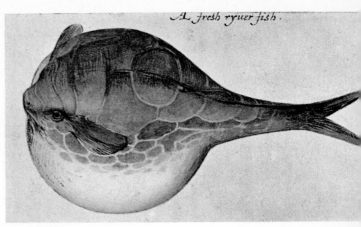

A fresh ryver fish.

A PUFFER, *which swells after being caught, is a common fish. White proba[bly] painted it to prove the New World would not be entirely alien to Englishm[en]*

A DOLPHIN *is rendered in fine detail by White, who painted the creatures [of] North America more realistically than he did the Indians who lived the[re]*

A LAND CRAB *is painstakingly, if somewhat inaccurately, depicted in this painting by White, who was a surprisingly good naturalist. The crab's eyes are drawn pointing outward; they actually should be angled inward.*

A lande Crab.

FISHERMEN AT WORK *make a haul in the t[idal] waters of North Carolina. In the canoe [(la-] beled "cannow" by White) one man padd[les,] another scoops up the quarry, while a m[an] and woman tend a fire that smokes the f[ish]*

The manner of their fishing.

A Cannow

SUPPER FOR TWO *for this man and his wife consists of boiled corn meal served in a solid wooden platter placed on a mat. The English attributed the longevity of the Indians to their practice of never eating or drinking to excess.*

THE CROPS AND FRUIT OF A FERTILE CONTINENT

The agricultural activities of the New World fascinated White. During his travels he made many stops at Caribbean islands, and he carefully drew the lush tropical fruit he found there. In Virginia he painted a number of pictures of farming communities such as Secoton *(right)*. The Indians at Secoton made three plantings of corn a year so that the harvests would be staggered. The fields were posted with watchmen in huts charged with making constant noise to frighten off animals and birds. The communal meals of corn, often combined with fish or venison, were served on long mats, the men sitting on one side, women on the other.

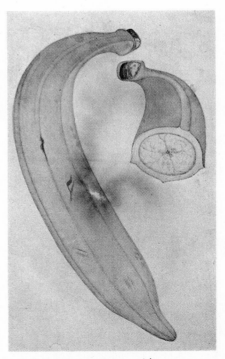

A HORN PLANTAIN, *a type of banana, was a new fruit the English found in the Caribbean.*

The place of Solem...

The house wherin the Tomb...

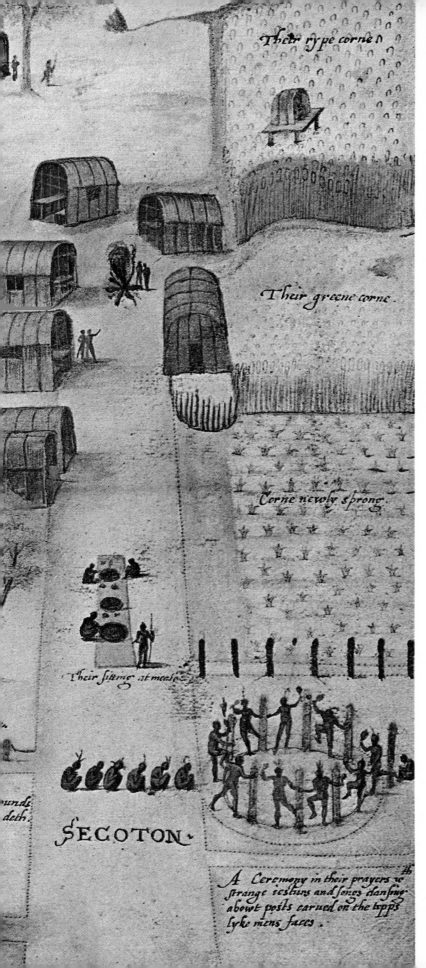

Their rype corne

Their greene corne.

Corne newly sprong.

Their sittinge at meate.

SEGOTON·

A Ceremony in their prayers ve strange iestures and songes dansinge abowt posts carued on the topps lyke mens faces.

A MAMMEE APPLE *resembles a common apple but is actually a tropical fruit with sweet flesh White saw in the West Indies.*

THE PINEAPPLE *was indigenous to the New World but the Europeans liked it and spread it to tropical areas around the globe.*

A FARM VILLAGE, *seen in a color plan, is labeled to show the corn fields, dining areas, prayer fire and ceremonial arena.*

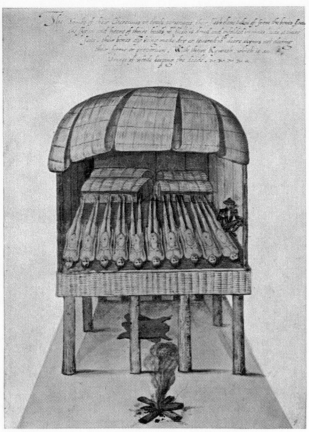

THE CORPSES OF THE CHIEFS *are laid out after being stripped of flesh and innards. A protective idol at right watches over them.*

THE CHRISTIANS VIEW THE INDIAN RELIGION

The English admired the cooperative nature of the Indian societies, but they were shocked at some of their religious practices. Under the Indian polytheism, tribal chiefs were held in esteem as gods, even after they died. Their bodies were placed on a platform in a large shelter *(above)* after their intestines and flesh had been removed and the skin replaced over the skeleton. The flesh was dried in the sun, wrapped in reed mats and put at their feet. Tribal sorcerers, highly respected because they were believed to be conversant with devils, lived with the chiefs' corpses and mumbled prayers near them day and night. In another ceremony, large celebrations were convened among tribes periodically, usually ending in exotic dances after sunset *(right)*.

A MYSTICAL DANCE *was part of an Indian feast attended by neighbori*

bes. Three virgins dance in the center while other dancers hop near tall poles carved with human heads. The dancers' back marks indicate their home villages.

7

"TERRA AUSTRALIS INCOGNITA"

BRITISH EXPLORER *Captain James Cook sailed three times to the South Pacific. On his voyages he mapped and described New Zealand and eastern Australia, which he claimed for England, and indicated the limits of Antarctica.*

In contrast to the Americas, which were not anticipated but did exist, Terra Australis Incognita was eagerly sought for but was a myth—the most stubborn myth in the history of exploration.

The Renaissance inherited from antiquity the notion that there existed a great unknown southern continent, usually designated on maps as Terra Australis Incognita. This belief arose from an instinct and a theory. The instinct was an abhorrence of a vacuum, an uneasy desire to put something solid amidst the vast waters south of the Tropic of Capricorn. The theory was that far to the south there must be a land mass large enough to balance the weight of the northern continents and thus prevent the world from turning upside down.

The concept was of little practical interest, however, until the Portuguese voyages around Africa showed that men could safely cross the equator without burning up. From that moment Terra Australis became something to reckon with; it could be reached, it might be valuable. Men began to speculate about its limits, inhabitants and wealth. They would continue to theorize for centuries.

At various times in its long history, the southern continent was thought to fill and cover the areas encompassing the whole Southern Hemisphere almost as far north as the equator. The voyages of Dias and Da Gama pushed its presumed boundary south of the Cape of Good Hope, and Magellan's circumnavigation pushed it below 52°—but only along his route. The unknown continent diminished only when a ship's keel passed over its outline as shown on existing maps.

The extraordinary persistence of this ghost continent resulted in great part from the practical difficulties involved in searching for it. In the 16th Century Spain and Portugal were the dominant powers in the Southern Hemisphere. Portugal was too busy maintaining contact with Brazil, India and the Moluccas to spare the ships and men needed for further exploration. Spain, on the other hand, with bases in Peru and Mexico, and a steady trade between Acapulco, on Mexico's west coast, and the Philippines, was in a good position to explore the South Pacific. But the southeast trade winds lifted ships steadily northward toward the equator and made it almost impossible for vessels leaving from

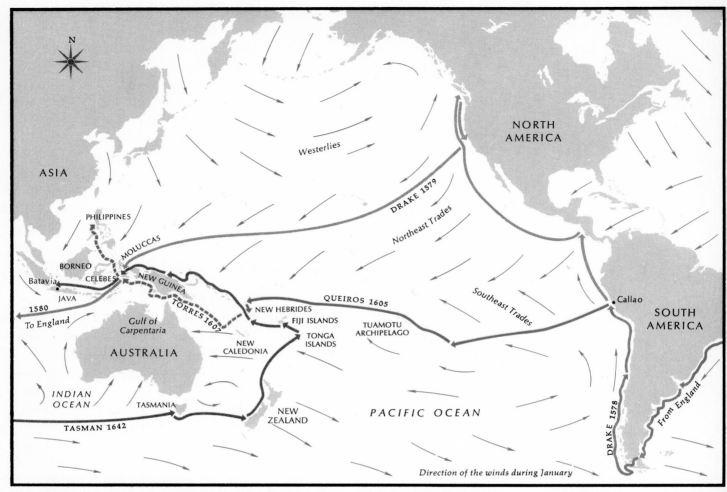

SEEKING THE SOUTHERN CONTINENT *called Terra Australis, three early navigators were carried by prevailing winds. Sir Francis Drake, after exploring the west coast of the Americas, caught the northeast trades to the Moluccas. Pero Fernandes de Queiros led an expedition from Peru to the New Hebrides; one of his* ships *sailed on to the Philippines (dotted line). Sailing before westerlies, Abel Tasman, a Dutchman, discovered Tasmania and New Zealand, which he thought to be the mythical continent's northern tip. None of these men ever solved the mystery of Terra Australis, which awaited explanation by Captain Cook in 1775.*

Mexico to enter the southern ocean. Nearly all the great exploring sweeps that were made deep into the South Pacific had to start from the west, around the Cape of Good Hope.

A further difficulty lay in the inadequacy of Renaissance navigation. The position of a landfall was rarely located accurately enough for it to be identified again. In large measure this reflected the mariners' inability to determine longitude with any degree of exactness. While dead reckoning is good enough to reach and identify the broad outlines of a mainland, islands are another matter. In 1568 the Spaniard Alvaro de Mendaña discovered the Solo-

mon Islands, some 200 miles east of New Guinea, so naming them because he assumed that they were the outriders of Terra Australis, in which he expected to find Solomon's fabled mines. Then the islands were lost. Mendaña himself could not find them on his second voyage. While the islands were later rediscovered several times—and on each occasion were given new names—they were not recognized as Mendaña's discovery for two centuries.

Lands mentioned by Marco Polo had also slipped down into Terra Australis. As explorers investigated the islands of Indonesia and the Malaysian coasts without finding kingdoms as wealthy as those Polo had described, map makers pushed these elusive realms a little farther south. There was the kingdom of Lokak, for instance, of which Polo had said: "Gold is so plentiful that no one who did not see it could believe it." Lokak was probably Thailand or Malaya; but since the Europeans found very little gold in these lands, Lokak was moved to the mysterious southern continent. In the immensely influential atlas published in 1570 by Abraham Ortelius of Antwerp, Terra Australis runs northwest from the Strait of Magellan, rising to a headland which would have included New Guinea, New Zealand and Australia—and the kingdom of Lokak.

This atlas was circulated in England, as were the rumors that the Spaniards had discovered Solomon's rich region of Ophir. Gradually, under the stimulus of imaginative merchants and of geographical experts like John Dee—who was as sure of Terra Australis as he was of the polar passages —plans took shape to explore the southern continent. The undertakings were on a grandiose scale: indeed, it was at this time that the phrase "British Empire" was first used by John Dee. Spain had the west, Portugal the east: England, Dee asserted, should have the south.

It was at this point that Francis Drake was called back from marauding in the Spanish Main and, in 1577, sent off on what turned out to be the first circumnavigation of the world since Magellan's voyage of 1519-1522. Drake's first set of instructions ordered him to pass through the Strait of Magellan and then find and follow the coast of Terra Australis. Then, having presented gifts to any rulers he came across, he was to retrace his journey through the Strait and return home. But before sailing these plans were changed; apparently Queen Elizabeth and her Secretary of State, Sir Francis Walsingham, both of them hardheaded political opportunists, had defeated the geographical idealists. The new—and secret—plan was for Drake to turn north

after passing the Strait and raid the coasts and shipping of Spanish Peru. At that latitude he would have little choice but to take the trade winds to the East Indies and then come home around Africa.

Drake, then, was to sail in no spirit of idealism or record-breaking. His voyage was a skirmish in the continuing cold war against Spain, and to prevent its purpose being known, his crew and the world were told that he was bound for a normal trading voyage to the Levant.

On December 13, 1577, Drake sailed from Plymouth in his flagship, the *Pelican* (renamed en route the *Golden Hind*), accompanied by four other ships. In an exact parallel with Magellan's misfortunes, Drake was deserted by one ship and had to settle a mutiny in Patagonia. After he had passed through the Strait of Magellan and entered the Pacific, storms battered him some way down the west coast of Tierra del Fuego. Looking southwest from these wild waters he concluded that Terra Australis was not there, a conclusion which was correct, but which was probably the consequence of his having decided not to look for it (his heart was certainly with the Queen's change of plan).

Drake's voyage to Panama, while it is celebrated in the annals of privateering, has nothing to do with exploration. The story that announced the Mediterranean as his destination had done its work; no Spaniard expected to see an English vessel in the Pacific. Drake looted on shore and captured at sea with all the ease of utter surprise. One of his crew recalled the occasion when "we found by the seaside a Spaniard lying asleep who had lying by him 13 bars of silver which weighed 4,000 ducats Spanish. We took the silver and left the man."

Farther north, at Lima, "being entered the haven, we found there about twelve sail of ships lying fast moored at an anchor, having all their sails carried on shore, for the masters and merchants were here most secure, having never been assaulted by enemies. . . . Our general rifled these ships." Still farther north, off Cape de San Francisco, the English came upon the treasure ship *Cacafuego*. They boarded her, and "found in her great riches, as jewels and precious stones, thirteen chests full of royals of plate, four score pound weight of gold and six and twenty tons of silver." Elizabeth had planned shrewdly: a *Cacafuego* in the hand was better than a Lokak in the bush.

From Panama, Drake cast well out to the west before turning north, and so was unable to disprove the common belief that California was an island. Ironically, while the original intention had been to discover the southern continent, the only piece of actual exploration Drake carried out was connected with the northwest passage. Proceeding up the west coast of America, farther north than anyone had sailed before, Drake established that the Strait of Anian, if it existed, must lie beyond modern Vancouver. Since the land at that point extended northwest, instead of northeast as it should have done according to the theorists, Drake gave up searching and turned south down the coast. In the neighborhood of San Francisco he stopped to refit his vessel, and took possession of New Albion, as he named the country. In all probability he saw it not so much as a future colony but as a way station for attempts to find the Pacific entrance to the northwest passage.

The run across to the Moluccas was uneventful, but once in the islands, in spite of Drake's superb handling of the ship against contrary winds among the shoals, the *Golden Hind* was nearly lost. A crew member described the incident: "Upon the 9 of January in the 1579 we ran suddenly upon a rock, where we stuck fast from 8 of the clock at night until 4 of the clock in the afternoon of the next day, being indeed out of all hope to escape the danger. But our general . . . showed himself courageous and of a good confidence. . . . We lightened our ship upon the rocks of 3 tons of cloves, 8 pieces of ord-

nance and certain meal and beans, and then the wind (as it were in a moment by the special grace of God) changing from the starboard to the larboard of the ship we hoisted our sails and the happy gale drove our ship off the rock into the sea again, to the no little comfort of all our hearts."

The rest of the voyage across the Indian Ocean and back through the Atlantic was relatively easy, and as the *Golden Hind* entered Plymouth harbor in September 1580 with the *Cacafuego*'s treasure, Drake's first question to the fishermen there was whether the Queen was still alive and well.

The next man to enter the story of the southern continent was of very different mettle from Drake. Terra Australis was, after all, a vision rather than a fact, and its quest required a visionary like Pero Fernandes de Queiros, who thought it was his destiny to find Terra Australis, bring its wealth to Spain and its peoples to Christ.

Queiros had accompanied Mendaña on the voyage of discovery to the Marquesas and the elusive Solomons, and this voyage had convinced him that the maps were right—that Terra Australis was just to the south of Mendaña's track. He was determined to discover the new continent, and though he was Portuguese by birth, like Magellan his principal service was under the Spanish flag.

Queiros started his campaign in 1600 by firing the enthusiasm of the Spanish ambassador in Rome and, through him, the pope. Then, in 1602, he went to Spain where he pressed his plan at court with such vigor that the Spanish Council of State, groaning under the weight of his petitions and memoranda, complained that Queiros thought he was a second Columbus. He certainly had as hard a task as had the Admiral to sell his vision to the Crown. In April 1603, Queiros finally secured authorization. With this in hand, he set off for South America, where he collected ships and crews, and set sail from Callao in Peru on December 21, 1605.

At the start, he headed south and west on a course that he calculated would give him a landfall on Terra Australis just below the Solomons, the island fringe of the continent. His route took him through a part of the Pacific more thickly strewn with islands than any previous explorer had encountered. He discovered Henderson Island and several of the islands in the Tuamotu Archipelago, the Duff group and several of the Banks Islands.

An expert navigator, Queiros discovered the northern New Hebrides on May 3, 1606, south and east of the Solomons, which was exactly where he intended to arrive. The largest of this group he assumed was the long-sought-for mainland. Once anchored in the great northern bay of the main island, Queiros took possession for the King of Spain of "all this region of the south as far as the Pole, which from this time shall be called Australia del Espiritu Santo." Exhorting his tough and truculent men not to ruin the virgin innocence of the new land with sin, he made plans to build a city, the New Jerusalem, on a river he named the Jordan. But his vision was short-lived. Four weeks later he was out at sea again and bound east across the Pacific for the Western Hemisphere. The reason for his sudden change of plan is not clear. He apparently was forced to leave either by a storm which burst into the bay or because his men were threatening mutiny unless he turned back.

Espiritu Santo was, of course, just an island. The chief contribution of Queiros' expedition actually was made by his second-in-command, Luis Vaz Torres. When Queiros left the harbor of Espiritu Santo, Torres was unsure whether his chief was off on a short reconnaissance or had gone for good. After waiting for some time, Torres sailed his own vessel west and south around New Guinea, through the strait (now bearing his name) that divides that island from Australia. With this pas-

sage he proved that Terra Australis, if it existed, did not there reach up further than latitude 10° south.

Although Torres' voyage lopped off one part of the mythical southern continent, the belief in Terra Australis as a whole was strengthened by Queiros' own reports. His real islands and imagined mainland did not tempt Spain, whose failing resources were already overcommitted, but cartographers seized on Queiros' descriptions. The islands he had discovered were marked "Seen by Queiros"; his thesis that they were the "children" of a "mother continent" appealed to geographers until well into the 18th Century. For the next century and a half voyagers in the South Pacific, infatuated by Queiros' theory, interpreted every new bank of low cloud or space of glass-calm water as a sign that they were in the vicinity of a mainland.

Up to this point, however, all the ships seeking Terra Australis had entered the Pacific from the east. The first incursions into this area from the west were made by the Dutch. In part this was because by the early 17th Century they had established conveniently situated bases in the East Indies. Another reason was that by the same period Dutch captains had adopted a new sailing route to the East. They no longer used the southwesterly winds of the monsoon to bring them from the Cape of Good Hope to the East Indies via India; now they kept the south, using the westerlies to take them from the Cape to the longitude of Java, at which point they turned north to the Indies. It was from Bantam in Java that Willem Janszoon left in 1605 to survey the south coast of New Guinea and then, sailing some way into the Gulf of Carpentaria, became the first European to discover Australia, which the Dutch called New Holland.

By 1642, when Abel Tasman made the first sustained attempt to discover the nature of New Holland, the Dutch had explored all of the west coast, fragments of the north coast, and the south coast as far east as longitude 133°. There was much uncertainty, however. The Dutch were still not aware that Torres had found a navigable strait between Cape York and New Guinea. The southern limit of the Gulf of Carpentaria was unexplored, and some thought that it led into a strait that made the whole of western Australia an island; it was conjectured that the land east of the presumed strait might be a giant promontory of Terra Australis.

Tasman sailed from Batavia (today's Jakarta) to Mauritius and then on down to 49° south before turning east and a little north. Thereafter he held his course, the waves from his bow washing away the possibility of Terra Australis in that quarter of the Indian Ocean. One afternoon he came upon "the first land we had met with in the South Sea." It was Tasmania, later to be named after him, and he sent the ship's carpenter swimming through the rough surf to take possession for the Dutch East India Company by erecting an inscribed pole. He did not realize that he had come upon an island, but by continuing to sail eastward he showed that New Holland itself was an island. Thus, through Tasman's findings, the southern continent was again vastly diminished in size.

On the other hand, when he struck New Zealand, Tasman thought that this was indeed a promontory of Terra Australia, which he imagined fell away southeastward towards Cape Horn. In a later voyage Tasman verified that the Gulf of Carpentaria was not a strait but a bay, although, like his predecessors, he was misled by the shoals and reefs of Torres Strait into thinking that northeastern Australia was connected with New Guinea.

After Tasman's voyage, interest in the inhospitable area around Australia languished for more than a century. Then, in 1766, the British Admiralty sent Samuel Wallis and Philip Carteret to discover Terra Australis, or, as the English scholar-propagandist Alexander Dalrymple preferred to put it, find it again, for after Queiros' and subsequent voyages Dalrymple felt that it was "impossible for anyone at this time to discover it." Wallis' orders were to round Cape Horn or go through the Strait of Magellan and then "stretch to the Westward . . . loosing as little Southing as Possible, in Search of the Land or Islands supposed to lie in that part of the Southern Hemisphere." If he found Terra Australis, he was to collect information about "the Genius, Temper and Inclinations of the Inhabitants of such Islands or Lands as you may Discover. . . . But if no Inhabitants are found on the Land or Islands so discovered, you are, in such case, to take Possession of such Land or Islands so discovered for His Majesty."

West of the Strait of Magellan, Wallis and Carteret were separated by a storm, Carteret taking the Swallow by a more southerly route, very close to Queiros' route. After discovering Pitcairn Island, he passed south of the Tuamotu Archipelago, noting that although his chart was marked at this point "land seen by Queiros," he did not see any signs of it. Because his crew was ill from scurvy he decided not to go to Espiritu Santo but to head for the Philippines for fresh food and rest.

Meanwhile Wallis had sailed through the middle of the Tuamotu Archipelago and onward to begin a legend of a different sort, for he discovered Tahiti. As George Robertson, master of Wallis' ship, the Dolphin, wrote: "This made us all rejoice. . . . We now looked upon ourselves as relieved from all our distresses, as we was almost certain of finding all sorts of refreshments on this great body of land." They were now certain, he concluded, that "we saw the long wished for Southern Continent."

Southern continent it was not, but it did provide the men with all sorts of refreshment, including the one for which it became most famous—its girls, the sight of whom "made all our men madly fond of the shore, even the sick which had been on the doctor's list for some weeks before." The price of an evening's pleasure was quickly worked out at one good-sized nail. An idyllic life began until one day, as Robertson recalled, "when I was ordering the liberty men into the boat the carpenter came and told me every cleat in the ship was drawn, and all the nails carried off. . . . the boatswain informed me that most of the hammock nails was drawn, and two thirds of the men obliged to lie on the deck for want of nails to hang their hammocks."

Though Wallis went on to discover some of the other Society Islands and Rongerik in the Marshalls, it is with Tahiti that his name will always be linked. In the annals of exploration he figures not as the man who failed to look seriously for a fabled continent but as the man who found a South Sea paradise.

Less than a year afterward, another explorer, the Frenchman Louis Antoine de Bougainville, appeared in Tahiti on April 6, 1768. From the moment he tried to lower his anchor he was confronted by the same charming problem. "In spite of all our precautions, one young woman came aboard onto the poop and stood by one of the hatches above the capstan . . . the young girl negligently allowed her loincloth to fall to the ground, and appeared to all eyes such as Venus showed herself to the Phrygian shepherd. She had the goddess' celestial form." Bougainville's feelings, like Robertson's, were mixed. "I ask; how could one keep at work, in the midst of such a spectacle, four hundred Frenchmen, young sailors who for six months had not seen a woman?"

Bougainville, after a blissful interlude in Tahiti, sailed westward again until he came to the New Hebrides. From there he continued to the west, determined to discover Terra Australis, which his map showed as protruding northwest towards New Guinea. By this time, provisions were running so low that Bougainville noted in his journal that "at supper we ate some rats, and found them very good." Nevertheless, Bougainville held to his course.

During the sweltering days that followed, there was one brief diversion from rats and worry. One of the sailors, who had caused general surprise by not being interested in the girls of Tahiti, turned out to be a girl herself, an orphan who had joined the expedition out of curiosity and a spirit of adventure. The disclosure may have complicated the rest of the voyage for her, but it establishes Jeanne Baré as the first woman known to have circumnavigated the world.

Keeping to his determined course—"Oh Bellin," sighed Bougainville, referring to the cartographer who interpreted Queiros so optimistically, "how much are you costing us?"—Bougainville eventually sighted the Great Barrier Reef of Australia. At last, and after much thought, he decided to turn north. "The consecutive appearance of these three sets of breakers," he noted, "does not allow me to continue to seek here the continent of Queiros. These approaches are in no way like those mentioned by that navigator."

Unwilling to put much trust in the existence of Torres Strait, Bougainville squeezed past the eastern extremity of New Guinea, passed that huge island's northern coast, and turned west again for the East Indies and, eventually, home to France. En route he met and passed Carteret's lumbering *Swallow*. "How he must have suffered in such a poor ship!" commented Bougainville in his journal. Within a few years, however, it was to be another Englishman with equally slow ships who was finally to settle the problem of Terra Australis in the course of two expeditions. The leader of these ventures was James Cook, his ships the *Endeavour* and the *Resolution*.

By the time of Cook's first voyage in 1768, successive explorations had confined Terra Australis to a location somewhere south of latitude 50°, somewhere east of Africa and somewhere west of Cape Horn. But its existence was accepted as a possibility by every geographer, and as a certainty by many. Among the many was Dalrymple. To Tasman's identification of New Zealand as part of Terra Australis, Dalrymple attached Queiros' assertion that there must be mainland south of all the islands he had seen, and he derived a continent that thrust itself far up in the South Pacific between New Zealand and Cape Horn.

Such a continent would not only be enormous, but it would contain climates ranging from the polar to the temperate; it would thus be suited to colonization and, in all probability, be rich in products profitable to European traders. Its discovery would seriously upset the pattern of power in Europe by turning the Pacific into the private lake of its possessor. It was essential, urged Dalrymple, that it should be occupied by England.

It so happened that a very rare event had been forecast for 1769: the transit of Venus across the face of the sun—a phenomenon that would not recur for a century. It was hoped that observations of this event from widely separated points would enable astronomers to work out the distance between the earth and the sun. Wallis' report of Tahiti caused the Royal Society, with the approval of King George III, to settle on Tahiti as the mid-Pacific observation site. When Cook sailed on August 25, 1768, it was with a double objective: to organize these observations, and then, according to secret instructions, to search for the southern continent which "there is reason to imagine . . . may be found to the southward of the tract lately made by Captain Wallis."

Cook was then in his 40th year, an experienced navigator and surveyor. He had helped to chart the shoals of the St. Lawrence River through which the British fleet worked its way to capture Quebec

A MAORI WOOD CARVING, *once used as a decorative pillar for a house, illustrates the skill of New Zealand's native artists at the time of Captain Cook's Pacific explorations. The Maoris, a gifted and tenacious people, had a highly developed, close-knit culture which helped them to survive European settlement, disease and New Zealand's later civil wars.*

in 1759 and had gained the respect of the Admiralty for the thorough way in which he had later carried out survey work on the coasts of Nova Scotia and Newfoundland. Keenly alive to the contributions of contemporary astronomers and instrument makers to navigation, he was better equipped to chart his progress than any earlier explorer. He also had an integrity and sense of purpose that were all the more respected by his men because of his intense care for their health: Cook was the first voyager to show that scurvy could be banished by cleanliness and a careful diet, the first captain to assume that it was possible to bring a ship's company home intact.

The *Endeavour* came into the Pacific via Cape Horn. After the observations had been made on Tahiti, Cook turned due south until he reached latitude 35°; then turning west, he held to that course in spite of the adverse westerlies. Raising the coast of New Zealand, he methodically surveyed its shores, thus detaching one more section from Terra Australis. He was not content with that. Although his ship badly needed repair, his crew was in better health than Europeans had ever been after so long a voyage, so Cook took the *Endeavour* on westward until he sighted the Australian coast.

Once more he patiently sounded, took sights and charted 2,000 miles of the Australian coast to add to his 2,400 miles of the New Zealand coastline. It was work that became increasingly perilous as he came within the Great Barrier Reef. On one of his charts, at latitude 16° south, just off Weary Bay, he marked a group of rocks with this inscription: "On these rocks the ship lay 23 hours." This laconic remark commemorates a day as hazardous as that spent in similar circumstances by Drake on the *Golden Hind.*

The *Endeavour* had been moving along the reef —the very sight of which had made Bougainville sheer off to the north—for weeks, and one night she stuck fast on a coral ledge at high tide—only minutes after the sounding line had shown 17 fathoms. Taking their cue from Cook's calm efficiency, the crew lightened the ship of guns and ballast and surplus stores, floated all the heavy spars overboard, and lowered boats to find deep water and good holding ground for anchors. When the tide was full next day, lines attached to the anchors were winched in but the ship would not move. Still there was no panic. The night tide was higher and the *Endeavour* floated clear; a sail was stretched under the hull where she had been holed, and Cook managed to scrape her over the bar to safety at the mouth of the river which still bears the name of his vessel.

Not long after this episode, Cook moved out into sea through a gap in the reef and sailed north. It was when the *Endeavour* closed once more with the reef to test the existence of the strait Torres had reported finding between Cape York and New Guinea that the greatest peril of all came. In his journal for August 16, 1770, Cook wrote that just before dawn "the roaring of the surf was plainly heard and at daybreak the vast foaming breakers were too plainly to be seen not a mile from us, towards which we found the ship was carried by the waves surprisingly fast. We had at this time not an air of wind and the depth of water was unfathomable so that there was not a possibility of anchoring." The small boats were lowered but their oarsmen could not tow the *Endeavour* against the force of the current.

"At this critical juncture," Cook wrote, ". . . a small air of wind sprung up. . . . With this and the assistance of the boats we could observe the ship to move off from the reef in a slanting direction, but in less than 10 minutes we had as flat a calm as ever. . . . We were not above 200 yards from the breakers." The chance of survival seemed slim until an opening was spotted in the reef about a mile

145

away. Although he desperately needed every ounce of pulling power, Cook gambled by sending off one of the small boats to investigate the gap. When the boat returned with a favorable report, "it was immediately resolved to try to secure the ship in it; narrow and dangerous as it was. . . . A light breeze soon after sprung up at ENE which with the help of our boats and a flood tide we soon entered the opening and were hurried through in a short time by a rapid tide." They were safe.

"Such are the vicissitudes," Cook noted, in words that sum up as graphically as any the spirit of exploration, "attending this kind of service and must always attend an unknown navigation. Was it not for the pleasure which naturally results to a man from being the first discoverer, even was it nothing more than sands and shoals, this service would be insupportable."

When Cape York was reached shortly afterward, Cook again did the difficult rather than the obvious thing. Instead of making eastward for the open sea he entered the shoals to the west and became the second man since Torres to sail through Torres Strait and the first to give general publicity to the fact that New Guinea was an island.

This first voyage accomplished much. But it was Cook's second voyage on the *Resolution* from 1772 to 1775 that gave the myth of Terra Australis its death blow. Profiting from his experience, Cook suggested that he should enter the Pacific from around Africa and so avoid the battle against the prevailing westerlies. In this way he could reach 40° south and below. The Admiralty agreed and directed him to go south from Cape Town and circumnavigate the globe in as southerly a latitude as he could hold. This Cook did, and even though he was plagued by ice he kept close to 60° most of the way and even penetrated the Antarctic Circle itself three times. "Thus," he said in his report on the voyage, "I flatter myself that the intention of the voyage has in every respect been fully answered, the Southern Hemisphere sufficiently explored and a final end put to the searching after a Southern Continent, which has at times engrossed the attention of some of the maritime powers for near two centuries past, and the geographers of all ages. That there may be a continent or large tract of land near the pole, I will not deny. On the contrary I am of the opinion there is."

Antarctica itself, the icy, unpopulated remnant of Terra Australis, still remained to be explored. But Cook's voyage demonstrated that whatever the southern continent consisted of, it nowhere reached latitudes where it would serve the purposes of 18th Century Europe.

Cook set off on his last voyage to the Pacific in 1776, and died an explorer's death on February 14, 1779. After an initially friendly welcome in Hawaii, the natives tired of the requisitions of food made by the Englishmen. Ultimately there was a heated quarrel in the course of which Cook was stabbed to death and cut into pieces by the furious Hawaiians.

Cook's legacy was immense. Trusting Cook's charts, cartographers rubbed the name of Queiros from their maps, and nations turned to pursuing their interests in friendlier waters. A new era of scientific exploration had begun, with knowledge, rather than conquest, as its goal.

Cook's voyages produced more reliable information about the nature of the world than those of any other explorer. Because of the accuracy of his observations, his pioneering care for the health of his men and his remarkable blend of daring and coolness, he is the earliest example of a new race of scientific explorers. But his science was devoted to investigating the myth that haunted the first Age of Exploration. He hinges the old exploration to the new; he closes a period that began with the discovery of a new continent by destroying the notion of an imaginary one.

THE COLORFUL JOURNALS OF CAPTAIN COOK

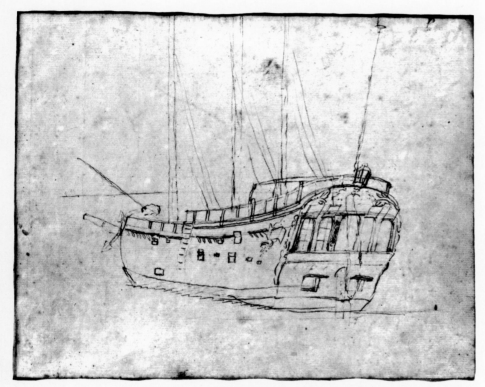

A sketch of the "Endeavour," Cook's most famous ship.

The talented Englishman James Cook covered more sea distance, discovered more new lands and contributed more to the sum of human knowledge than any explorer of his time. He was no swashbuckling mariner; it was his quiet competence, in fact, that made him such a brilliant explorer. In an age when family lineage still counted in the British navy, Cook was one of the first self-made men. A onetime grocer's apprentice, he joined the navy as a seaman and was a master within two years. The biographer James Boswell marveled that this "grave, steady man," who had as "wife a decent, plump Englishwoman . . . was preparing to sail round the world." But Cook did, and in the process proved that he was not only a superb seaman and commander but a perceptive scientific observer as well. On each of his three voyages he took along at least one scientist and one artist; in addition he kept a detailed journal of his own. His volumes of personal records meticulously report his epic voyages, which spanned 11 years and hundreds of thousands of miles; excerpts from these journals constitute a guide to some of the most fascinating adventures in the history of exploration.

FIRST VOYAGE: SCIENCE AND DISCOVERY

On his initial journey (1768-1771), Cook sailed south around Cape Horn, touching at Tierra del Fuego, then went on to Tahiti. Seeking the legendary Southern Continent, he found New Zealand and Australia instead and—surviving a near-shipwreck—charted their coasts.

Tierra del Fuego January 11-16, 1769

At 8 a.m. Saw the Land of Terra del Fuego. The Tide made Strong against us and the wind not abating caused a very great sea. I thought that Anchoring would be attended with risk. However I sent a Boat a Shore. [It] return'd bringing several Plants, Flowers &ca, most of them unknown in Europe. Hoisted the Boat in and made sail.

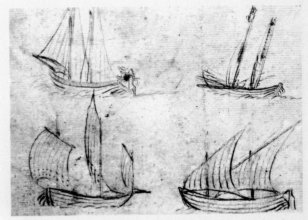

"Endeavour's" three cutters and (at bottom left) her longboat.

Hoisted out the Boats and Moor'd. While this was doing I went a Shore to look for a Watering place and to speak with the Natives assembled on the Beach to the number of 30 or 40. Their Hutts are made like a behive and open on one side where they have their fire.

These "beehive homes" sheltered Tierra del Fuegans from the cold of their homeland, only 790 miles from the Antarctic Circle.

[The huts] are made of small Sticks and cover'd with branches of trees, long grass &ca that are neither proff against wind, hail, rain or snow. These People live chiefly on shell fish such as Muscles. Their arows are bearded some with glass, several pieces of [which] we saw amongst them with other European things, which I think proves that they must sometimes travel to the Northward, as we know of no ship that hath been in those parts for years, besides they were not surprised at our fire arms. They have no boats that we saw, or any thing to go upon the water with. We could not discover that they had any head or chief, or Government [or] any necessary Utentials except it be a Bagg or Basket to gather Their Muscles into: in a Word they are perhaps as miserable a set of People as are this day on Earth.

Tierra del Fuegans huddle around a fire.

South Pacific waters March 23- April 7, 1769

A Tropicbird, or "bo'sun bird," sketched from Cook's ship.

PM. Saw some men of war Birds and Egg Birds and in the Morning saw more Egg Birds and Tropic Birds. Neither [the Egg Birds] nor the Man of War Birds are ever reckoned to go very far from land. . . . At Noon saw a Bird like Gannet. . . . A fresh trade wind and fine pleasent weather. At Noon saw a large flock of Birds, they had brown backs and white bellies, they fly and make a noise like Stearings and are shaped like them only some thing larger. Saw likewise some black sheer waters and several Men of War Birds. . . . At ½ past 6 AM, saw a small Island to the northward. There is some wood upon it but no Inhabitants but birds and for this reason is call'd Bird Island.

Tahitian faces and hairdress, as seen by one of Cook's artists.

[The Tahitians'] persons are of various colours. Those of the inferior sort who are much exposed to the sun are very dark brown. The Superiors who spend most of their time under shelter are not. Nay, some of the women are almost as fair as Europeans. Their hair is almost universally black, and this the women wear short. They have fine white teeth and for the most part short flat noses and thick lips. Their behaviour to strangers and to each other is open and courtious and from all I could see free from threachery, only they are theives.

The Houses are seperate each from the other and always in the woods and are without walls so that the air cooled by the shade of the trees has free access. The roofs are supported by rows of pillors or posts and neatly cover'd with thatch made of palm leaves. I have said that the houses are without walls but this is only in general for many of them are wall'd with wickerding but not so Close but to admit a free circulation of air.

A Tahitian family prepares a meal outside a long house on the plantation of a chief. Ironwood and banana trees grow nearby.

When one considers the tools these people have to work with, one cannot help but admire their workmanship. They have Adzes and small hatchets of hard stone. Chisels or gouges [are] made of human bones, generally the bone of the fore arm, but spike nails have pretty well supplied the place of these. With these ordinary tools that a European workman would expect to break the first stroke, I have seen them work surprisingly fast. To plane or polish their work they rub upon it with a smooth stone, Coral beat small and mixt with water.

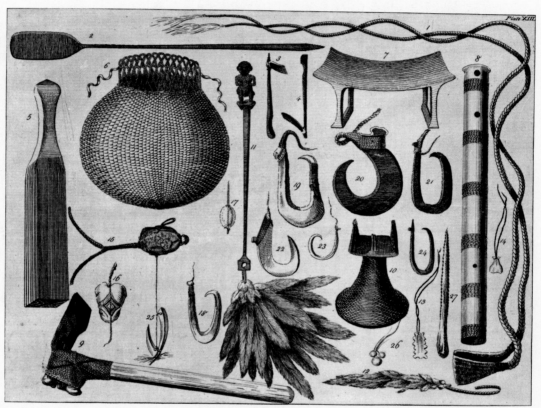

Tahitian utensils include: (1) sling; (2) paddle; (3) tattooing instrument—plus other tools and household equipment.

Breadfruit remains in season only 8 or 9 months and as it is the chief support of the inhabitants, a reserve must be made for months when they are without it. To do this the fruit is laid in heaps where it undergoes fermentation. The core is then taken out and the rest of the fruit thrown into a hole. Here it undergoes a second fermentation and will keep good for 10 or 12 Months. To use it they make it into balls which they wrap in leaves and bake. In this state it will keep good a Month or six Weeks.

The breadfruit plant is a Tahitian staple.

Maoris of New Zealand brandish weapons of war in a long canoe.

In the Morning several Canoes came to us from all Parts of the Bay; in them were about 130 or 140 People. To all appearances their first design was to attack us, being all compleatly Arm'd. However after Parading about the Ship near three hours, some times trading with us and at other times tricking of us, they disperse'd but not before we had fired a few Musquets. It is a little strange that with such a warlike people no weapons are found among them such as Bows and Arrows, Slings &ca. The Arms they use are Long spears or lances, a Staff about 5 feet long. They handle all their arms with great Agility.

The Natives of the Country are a well made Active people. They seem to injoy a good state of hilth and many of them live to a good old age. Many of the old and some of the middle aged men have their faces mark'd or tatoow'd with black and some few we have seen who have had their buttocks, thighs and other parts of their bodies mark'd but this is less common. The figures they mostly use are spirals drawn and connected together with great nicety and judgment. From this I conclude that it takes perhaps years to finish the operation. The manner in which it must be done must certainly cause intolerable pain.

Tattooed swirls on a Maori warrior's leg.

Saw two small islands and hauld off shore. A few Minutes before 11 the Ship Struck. We found that we had got upon a reef of Coral. The ship being quite fast we throw'd over board our guns, Iron and stone ballast, Casks, Hoops, staves, oyle Jars, decay'd stores &ca. About 20 past 10 oClock the Ship floated, we having at this time 3 feet 9 Inches water in the hold. . . . At 8 hauld her bow close a shore which gave us an opportunity to examine the leak. The whole was cut away as if by a blunt edge tool. A large piece of Coral rock was sticking in one hole and several pieces of fothering [caulking], small stones, sand &ca had stoped the water.

The "Endeavour," damaged on a reef off Australia, is beached on the bank of a river later named for her. Repairs took some six weeks.

I sent 3 Men into the Country to shoot Pigeons, as some few of these birds had been seen flying about. They returned with about half a dozen. One of the men saw an animal. It was of a Mouse Colour very slender and swift of foot. I saw this morning one of the Animals. It was the full size of a grey hound and shaped like one, with a long tail which it carried like a grey hound. I should have taken it for a wild dog, but for its walking or running in which it jumped like a Hare or a dear. Excepting the head and ears which was something like a Hare's, it bears no sort of resemblance to any European Animal I ever saw. [Later] we din'd of the animal & thought it excellent.

The creature the natives called "kanguru."

SECOND VOYAGE: ICE AND ISLANDERS

On his second trip (1772-1775), Cook made three deep probes into the Antarctic, and proved that there was no inhabited continent there, only ocean and ice. Wintering to the north, he swept the Pacific, exploring Easter Island, the New Hebrides and many other island groups.

In Antarctic waters December 12-30, 1772

Pass'd Six Islands of Ice this 24 hours. Some Gentlemen on Deck saw some Penguins. Snow and Sleet all the 24 Hours, the Thermometer generally below or at the freezing point so that our Sails and Rigging were chequered with Ice. Pass'd 18 more Islands of Ice, and saw some more Penguins. These Penguins differ only in some Minute particular from those found in other parts of the World. Their progression in the Water is however different to any I have seen. Instead of swimming like other Birds, they leap or scip something like the Fish known to Seamen by the Name of scip Jacks.

An Antarctic penguin, seen on an ice floe.

In Antarctic waters January 9, 1773

Cook's seamen gather ice for drinking water.

Finding loose pieces of Ice about, we hoisted out three Boats and took up as much as yeilded about 15 Tons of Fresh Water. We were obliged to break them with our Ice Axes before they could be taken into the Boats. The Salt Water that adhered to the pieces was so trifleing as not to be tasted and after they had laid on Deck a little while entirely drained off. The Melting of the Ice is a little tideous, otherwise this is the most expeditious way of Watering I ever met with.

New Zealand
March 27, 1773

We found we have only one man on board that can be called ill of this disease [scurvy]. My first care after the Ship was moored was to send a Boat & People a-fishing. Some

A spiny fish, native to New Zealand, as painted by one of the expedition's naturalists.

of the gentlemen went to a rock on which were many seals, one of which they killed. The fishing Boat was equally as successful by returning with as much fish as all hands could eat for supper and in a few hours in the morning supplied us with a Dinner. This gave us certain hopes of being Plentifully supplied with fish.

New Hebrides
August 6, 1774

After the Ship was moor'd I landed with a strong party of Men without any opposition being made by a great number of islanders, arm'd with darts, clubs, slings, bows and arrows. After our men were drawn up upon the beach I distributed to the old people presents of pieces of Cloth, Medals &ca, and ordered two Casks of Water to be fill'd out of a Pond. We got from them a few Cocoa-nuts but they would not part with any of their Arms which they held in constant readiness. Little was wanting to make them attack us, however our embarqueing probably disconcerted their scheme and after that they retired.

Cook and a party of his men land at Tanna, a volcanic island in the New Hebrides, while armed natives watch them menacingly.

THIRD VOYAGE: TAHITI, HAWAII—AND DEATH

On his final expedition (1776-1780), Cook returned to his favorite Tahiti, discovered Hawaii, sailed north to explore Alaska and the Bering Strait, then south again to Hawaii. There he was hailed as a god—but, at the peak of his career, was killed in a scuffle with the natives.

Friendly Islands May 16, 1777

Boxers challenge each other at Hapaee, in the Friendly Islands.

At day-break we steered for Hapaee. Upon landing, I saw a large concourse of people. Presently, a number of men entered, armed with clubs. These paraded about, and then they successively entertained us with single combats. One champion, stepping forward from one side, challenged those of the other side, by expressive gestures more than by words. If the challenge was accepted, the two combatants put themselves in proper attitudes and began. Some received blows which they must have felt for some time after.

Tahiti September 1, 1777

A man [was] to be sacrificed. The unhappy victim seemed to be a middle-aged man; and one of the lowest class of the people. They generally make choice of guilty persons or else of common, low, fellows, who stroll about without any fixed abode. We were told that he had been knocked on the head with a stone. Those who are [elected] to suffer are never apprized of their fate, till the blow is given.

Costumed dancers entertain in a Tahitian play.

The explorers observe human sacrifice in Tahiti.

We had an opportunity of observing one of their public *heevas*, or plays, in which [the king's] sisters appeared. Their dress on this occasion was picturesque and elegant; and they acquitted themselves in a very distinguished manner; though some comic interludes, performed by four men, seemed to yield greater pleasure to the audience. A sort of delicacy and whiteness distinguish the inhabitants. Their women struck us as possessing all those delicate characteristics which distinguish them from the other sex in many countries. The muscular appearance, so common amongst the Friendly Islanders, and which seems a consequence of their being accustomed to much action, is lost here, where the superior fertility of their country enables the inhabitants to lead a more indolent life.

An Indian girl from Prince William Sound.

The natives wear the hair cropt round the neck but the women allow it to grow long; and most tie a small lock of it on the crown. Both sexes have the ears perforated with holes, in which they hang bunches of beads. The Septum of the nose is also perforated; through which they thrust the quill feathers of small birds. But the most unsightly ornamental fashion is their having the under-lip slit, or cut through. This incision becomes so large as to admit the tongue through.

On the ice lay a prodigious number of sea-horses [walrus]; and, as we were in want of fresh provisions, the boats were sent. Some being always upon the watch, these, on the approach of the boat, would wake those next to them; and the whole herd would be awake presently. After they had been once fired at, they would tumble into the sea, in the utmost confusion.

Captain Cook's voyagers, hungry for fresh meat, hunt walrus in icy Arctic waters.

Houses in Unalaska were built partly below ground; a roof opening let in light.

These [islanders] are lousy and filthy in their houses. Round the sides of the huts, the families (for several are lodged together) have their separate apartments, where they sleep, and sit at work in a kind of trench. This is kept tolerably decent. But the middle of the house, common to all families, is a receptacle for dirt.

At 11 o'clock in the forenoon we anchored in thirteen fathoms of water in the bay which is called by the natives Karakakooa. The ships [became] much crowded with natives, and were surrounded by a multitude of canoes. I had nowhere, in the course of my voyages, seen so numerous a body of people assembled at one place. Besides those who had come off to us in canoes, all the shore of the bay was covered with spectators, and hundreds were swimming round the ship like shoals of fish. We could not but be struck with the singularity of this scene.

Captain Cook (center right) is killed by angry Hawaiians. They dismembered his body but later contritely returned it for sea burial.

This was the final entry in Cook's journal. A month later, in this very place, he was killed in an encounter with natives suspected of thievery. As James King, one of his lieutenants, described it: "An accident happened which gave a fatal turn. The boats, having fired at some canoes, killed a chief. The [islanders] armed themselves and a general attack followed. Our unfortunate Commander was stabbed in the back, and fell with his face in the water. His body was immediately dragged onshore and surrounded by the enemy, who...showed a savage eagerness to share in his destruction. Thus fell our great and excellent Commander!"

8

THE WORLD TAKES SHAPE

The Age of Exploration flowed imperceptibly into the era of colonization that followed. Even had the Europeans been aware that a new era was beginning, they were too busy with the problems of settlement to stop to consider what had been accomplished. Seen in the perspective of the centuries, however, the achievements of the era of exploration appear overwhelming.

The major accomplishment, of course, was the discovery of new lands many times greater in extent than Europe itself—and someday to become even more powerful than the home continent. In addition the era saw the development of systematic exploration; the disentanglement of geographic fact from age-old myth—a process which necessitated a major break with medieval patterns of thought; the modification of a good deal of medieval religious, political and social dogma; alterations in Europe's traditional diet with the discovery of new foods; and, as a long-term result, the realignment of political power in Europe.

In all this, the key figure was, of course, the explorer himself. What sort of man was he? Thomas More's *Utopia*, published in 1516, contains what might be considered the earliest literary portrait of one of these adventurous men—fictionalized, but clearly based on fact. The book tells of the travels of one Raphael Hythlodaeus, and particularly of his experiences on the island of Utopia (from the Greek meaning "no place"), where all the evils that afflict mankind, such as poverty and war, have been minimized.

Raphael, we are told, is "a man of advanced years, with sunburned countenance and long beard and cloak hanging carelessly from his shoulder, while his appearance and dress seemed to me to be those of a ship's captain." A Portuguese, Raphael had "joined Amerigo Vespucci and was his constant companion in the last three of those four voyages . . . but on the final voyage he did not return with him. He importuned and even wrested from Amerigo permission to be one of the twenty-four who at the farthest point of the last voyage were left behind. . . . And so he was left behind that he might have his way, being more anxious for travel than about the grave." From the Western Hemisphere, More recounts, Raphael made his way round the

TWO LADIES OF GOA, *a Portuguese colony on the west coast of India, greet a European suitor in this watercolor made in 1628. The caption, in old Portuguese, reads, "Unmarried Ladies—Indian and Christian." Portuguese men frequently married Indian girls who had been converted to Christianity.*

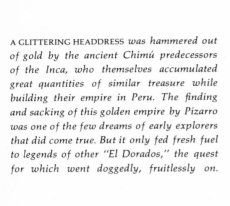

A GLITTERING HEADDRESS *was hammered out of gold by the ancient Chimú predecessors of the Inca, who themselves accumulated great quantities of similar treasure while building their empire in Peru. The finding and sacking of this golden empire by Pizarro was one of the few dreams of early explorers that did come true. But it only fed fresh fuel to legends of other "El Dorados," the quest for which went doggedly, fruitlessly on.*

world via Calicut to Portugal, discovering Utopia en route.

Since More was a contemporary of many of the great explorers, it is easy to assume that he may have drawn his bearded voyager from actual observation. But how closely did this imaginary traveler correspond to real Renaissance explorers? Did the men who opened the sea lanes to Asia and the Americas share Raphael's thirst for knowledge and his conviction that Europe had much to learn from peoples thousands of miles from their shores?

The two types of men who journeyed to distant places in the Renaissance—the individual traveler and the explorer who commanded expeditions—had distinctly different personalities. But there were some explorers, like Columbus, who preserved something of the romantic attitude of the independent tourist. And there were solitary wanderers, like the Jesuit Benedict de Goes, the traveler in western China, who displayed the explorer's determination to add to the sum of knowledge. This mixture of attitudes was not uncommon, and it accounts both for the way Renaissance travelers and explorers felt about what they discovered and for the manner in which the many things they found

colored the reactions of European stay-at-homes.

Attitudes changed during the Age of Exploration. In the first place, there was a shift from verification to objective observation. Instead of bending the observed facts to fit their preconceptions (as Vasco da Gama who, anticipating finding Christians in India, insisted that the Hindu temple he visited in Calicut was a church), the later voyagers came to examine and accept what was actually seen, regardless of the violence done to old beliefs.

In the second place, in their attitude toward strange peoples Renaissance men turned from condescension to comparison. They no longer held all native cultures in contempt, but realized that they had something to learn by comparing indigenous customs with the European way of life.

These changes represented one of the era's clearest shifts from late-medieval to modern ways of thought. Fortunately for posterity, there survive copious reports that make it possible to follow the shifts in opinion. Thus, a comment written in 1554 by the Englishman Richard Chancellor is a model of detachment, far removed from the condescension of the earliest explorers. Chancellor, second-in-command of Hugh Willoughby's expedition in search of a northeast passage, addressed his countrymen: "It is meet and necessary for all those that mind to take in hand the travel into far or strange countries, to endeavour themselves not only to understand the orders, commodities, and fruitfulness thereof, but also to apply them to the setting forth of the same whereby it may encourage others to the like travel."

None of this is to say, of course, that centuries-old prejudices and superstitions disappeared from European minds overnight. Many legends that had not been disproved persisted for years, exercising a continuing—and in some respects salutary—influence on exploration. An example is the myth of Prester John, which played a powerful role in encouraging men to penetrate Africa.

On the other hand, the belief that there were always better or more amazing things a little farther on often deflected men's attention from the novelties under their eyes. Reared on the detailed descriptions and startling illustrations of misshapen men and other monstrous oddities chronicled in the 14th Century writings of Sir John Mandeville, voyagers insisted on hunting for these imaginary creatures even while wonders of a more mundane variety greeted them at every turn.

The Mandevillian monsters continued to handicap progress toward a truly scientific outlook for centuries. For instance, as late as 1595 Sir Walter Raleigh returned from the Guiana coast of South America, which he had explored in search of El Dorado, and wrote: "Next unto Arui there are two rivers, Atoica and Caora, and on that branch which is called Caora, are a nation of people, whose heads appear not above their shoulders; which though it may be thought a mere fable, yet for mine own part I am resolved it is true. . . . Such a nation was written of by Mandeville, whose reports were holden for fables many years, and yet since the East Indies were discovered, we find his relations

true of such things as heretofore were held incredible." Despite Raleigh's assertions, the East Indies had not provided verification of Mandeville's tales. Nevertheless, Raleigh accepted the existence of Mandeville's monsters and firmly located them in imaginary South American landscapes.

To confuse reality still more there was the explorers' tendency to overpraise what they had found. They made their discoveries as glamorous and attractive as possible to justify their expeditions to canny sponsors and suspicious rivals.

This habit, strong in Columbus, was equally marked in Raleigh. Since his reputation depended on finding gold on the Orinoco, he described that river's valley in one of the most inviting passages in the whole range of travelers' prose. "I never saw a more beautiful country, nor more lively prospects, hills so raised here and there over the valleys, the river winding into divers branches, the plains adjoining without bush or stubble . . . the deer crossing in every path, the birds towards the evening singing on every tree with a thousand several tunes . . . the air fresh with a gentle Easterly wind, and every stone that we stooped to take up, promised either gold or silver by his complexion."

As it turned out, Raleigh had indeed found gold, though his enemies' machinations deprived him of credit for this discovery. In other ways, however, Raleigh—no doubt believing in the truth of his description—was deflected from exact observation by three things: his wish to impress, his memories of Mandeville, and his conviction that somewhere up-river lay the empire of the gilded man, El Dorado.

There is an explanation for this bewildering tendency of Renaissance travelers and explorers to mix exaggeration with objectivity. Although the new outlook of Italian humanism was beginning to influence European thinking, medieval attitudes were still widely prevalent—and the medieval mind was seldom incisive. When medieval man was confronted with an object his reaction was not (as is ours) to describe it in terms of itself—its dimensions, texture, color—but to associate it with something else. Allegory, moralizing, analogy: all these devices were used by medieval man—and by early Renaissance man, too—to ease the shock of seeing something new in its own right. The Age of Exploration, by exposing more people to more new objects than had ever been discovered before, challenged this impulse to think by association.

Progress through science and technology—in fact through all activities that led to the deliberate betterment of life—depended on the ability to say "that is that," not "that reminds me of something else." But the change did not come easily. For instance, when Simone Sigoli, a 15th Century Florentine, saw his first giraffe, he described it as "almost like an ostrich save that its chest has no feathers but has very fine white wool . . . it has horse's feet and bird's legs . . . it has horns like a ram."

The impulse to fragment, rather than consolidate a general impression, persisted well into the 16th Century. Pigafetta, in his chronicle of Magellan's around-the-world expedition, described the penguins and seals he saw in the Strait of Magellan in terms of geese and wolves. As late as 1555, an English description by Richard Eden of the head of an African elephant on display in London shows the typical late-medieval mixture of observation sidetracked by pious wonder and the acceptance of classical legend: "I saw it, and beheld it, not only with my bodily eyes, but much more with the eyes of my mind and spirit, considering by the work the cunning and wisdom of the workmaster. . . . Pliny and Solinus write that [elephants] use no adultery. If they happen to meet with a man in wilderness, being out of the way, gently they will go before him and bring him into the plain way."

By the end of the 16th Century, however, the standard of objective description was improving.

Eventually, most educated men discarded medieval thought processes. This was the dawn of modern scientific methodology, in which men attempt to establish factual explanations by means of observation, hypothesis and experiment.

When great issues were involved, unconscious falsification could still distort things seen or heard, as in Raleigh's description of Guiana. But neat and meticulous accounts became routine, as witness this 1597 description of a Japanese sandal by a Florentine traveler: "Their shoes are made entirely of a single straw sole of strands twined together, or perhaps of leather, with a thong fastened to the ends of both sides of the sole, which comes up over the foot. And there is also another strand that is joined to the first one mentioned, but is fastened . . . so that it may pass through the opening between the two large fingers of the foot. And thus that shoe or sole is held firmly on the foot. And when they want to remove it, they have only to raise their heel a little and shake the foot, which quickly slides out."

Along with this improvement in Europeans' skill at describing things accurately, there was an increased ability to compare and contrast native societies—their laws, marriage customs, food and religion—with the strikingly different European ways. Gradually the native peoples were seen not just as intelligent animals or as museum specimens, but as humans worthy of serious examination.

On the whole, Europeans effected a disastrous change in the pattern of life of native societies. The Spaniards made the Arawak Tainos of the West Indies work harder than their physiques could stand. When Columbus first encountered these gentle people, there were about 300,000 of them. Less than 60 years later perhaps 500 still survived in the islands. The French in North America induced primarily meat-eating hunter tribes like the Algonquins to change to a diet based on grain, which harmed

A BIZARRE HIPPOPOTAMUS, *painted by a 16th Century Austrian artist, looks like a thickset horse with a grotesque dog's head. The painter may have read a description of this strange animal by an explorer who actually saw one in Africa. But, like other Europeans of his day, he could not visualize the mysterious creature except in terms of animals he knew. Later explorers helped change such an associative, romantic approach to more precise scientific observation.*

their digestion; to this the French added alcohol, which further contributed to the downfall of the Indians.

Along with European work habits and diets came diseases. Lacking acquired immunities, natives died in tens of thousands from smallpox and from the fierce strains of venereal disease—whose origin remains uncertain—which were spread by lusty European sailors. The Portuguese made Brazilian converts wear clothes. The resulting changes in skin temperature made them suddenly vulnerable to pulmonary disease and thousands died.

To this more-or-less involuntary cruelty, Europeans added deliberate savagery. A German, Ambrose Alfinger, exploring Venezuela in 1530, bound his Indian porters together with a chain bolted to iron rings clamped round their necks. If a slave was too exhausted to carry on, his head was cut off to avoid the delay of removing the collar. Alfinger himself was finally killed by enraged Indians. In the lovely Marquesas Islands of the South

Pacific, one of Queiros' men shot a native who, in fear, had jumped into the sea, a child in his arms. The sailor explained "that he acted as he did lest he should lose his reputation as a good marksman."

The explorers were generally less cruel than the soldiers of fortune and settlers who came later, probably because their contacts with natives were briefer. However, episodes like Da Gama's deliberate and pointless firing of a ship containing women and children are salutary reminders that cruel punishments and cruel sports were part of life in Renaissance Europe, and that to most explorers the killing of a non-Christian was more like stamping out vermin than it was like murder.

Relations with native populations, miserable almost from the first, were further compromised by the institution of slavery. Again, it should be remembered that Europe took slavery for granted throughout the Middle Ages. Even in 15th Century Italy, slaves from Africa or southern Russia were common in rich families, and Italian merchants conducted a regular trade in boy slaves from the Balkans to serve in the armies of Turkey and Egypt. Columbus did not think twice about sending inhabitants of the West Indies back to Spain to become slaves.

Later, as the Spaniards began to mine for gold and silver in Mexico and Peru, and as the Portuguese built up their sugar plantations in Brazil, many strong workers had to be imported; Indians were unable to survive the grueling labor. So began the transatlantic trade in Negro slaves from West Africa, one of the most profitable sidelines of the Age of Exploration. One particularly grisly incident in this inhuman business involved French interlopers on the Brazilian coast. To strengthen themselves against the Portuguese, the Frenchmen were anxious to secure an alliance with local cannibal tribes; as an inducement, they imported West African Negroes for the Brazilian Indians to eat.

A start at anthropology emerged both from slavery and from European contact with native populations. Slave traders were forced to study the habits of different African tribes in order to select the most suitable laborers. Europeans were particularly intrigued by nakedness or near-nakedness. Equally fascinating were sexual customs such as polygamy. Columbus, though he helped destroy the Tainos, was so beguiled by their customs that he recorded them with some care, and thus bequeathed an invaluable source of information about this people. Cabral's companion, Pedro Vaz de Caminha, composed a remarkably exact portrait of the Brazilians he saw in 1500. Fernão Veloso, one of Vasco da Gama's men, persuaded his chief to let him spend some time with the inhabitants of the Cape of Good Hope in order to see how they lived and what they ate.

By the beginning of the 17th Century, the Italian trader and globetrotter Francesco Carletti was complaining of the loss to knowledge caused by the

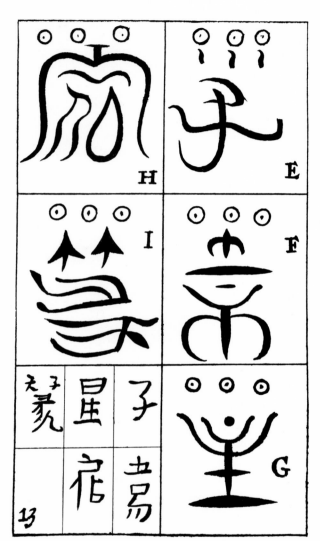

CHINESE CHARACTERS *were studied by missionaries so they could better understand Chinese thinking and thus win more converts. The Jesuit Athanasius Kircher determined that ancient figures (seen here in the large boxes) were a form of picture writing from which modern characters (lower left) descended (e.g., the characters at upper right in both large and small boxes correspond). Both groups spell out, "the letters of the plants and stars."*

indiscriminate cruelty of the Spaniards in the New World. Carletti pointed out that he could write more fully about the East Indies "because the Castilians had not imposed their yoke there."

It was religion, however—more than exploration and trade, more even than the needs of secular administration and settlement—that forced Europeans, through trial and error, to understand how other peoples lived and thought. Until the middle of the 16th Century, missionaries were full of hope that the newly discovered peoples could be converted to Christianity and made as nearly as possible into Europeans. These zealous Churchmen did not stop to consider that the different habits and different methods of social organization they encountered were the result of centuries of conditioning, nor did they realize how totally different other religious systems could be from their own. Flushed with excitement when whole tribes of Africans came willingly to be baptized, missionaries did not see at first that these converts were merely taking the precaution of placating the witch doctors from Europe. In African terms, there was no harm in adding the new type of magic to their own.

So long as missionaries did not speak the native languages fluently, they had considerable success. So eager were some of the new Christians that in 1518 a Negro bishop was consecrated in the Congo. But when Portuguese priests became skilled enough in local tongues to convey the idea that Christians had to be kind to their enemies—and, still worse, were only allowed one wife—enthusiasm waned among the Africans. Moreover, the growing ability of priests to communicate the social doctrines of Christianity coincided with a brisker traffic in slaves. Affronted by these developments, the majority of African Christians returned to their old gods.

Missionaries did better among the Indians of Brazil and Paraguay. The priests began badly by choosing the Tupi word for thunder as the word for God, thinking that the reverent looks with which this word was greeted meant that it was the Indian word for divinity. In fact it stood for the thunder demon, a redoubtable but wholly unsympathetic deity. Once this mistake had been rectified matters went more smoothly, and though the Indians needed the constant presence of missionary priests to keep them from moral lapses, they passively accepted the new religion. However, the missionaries had learned the important lesson that Christian teaching had to be modified in order to reach people whose habits of thought were remote from those of Europeans.

Through the missionary enterprise that followed exploration, in brief, Europeans learned to tolerate, and at certain points to respect other cultures. This was particularly true in Asia, where missionaries were forced first to distinguish between a host of well-established religions—Buddhism, Hinduism, Shintoism and their many variants—and then to modify their own European habits and attitudes in order to be accepted as trustworthy mentors. This was a hard lesson to learn. When St. Francis Xavier first visited Japan in 1549 he thought that since the local inhabitants were intelligent it would be easy to persuade them to accept Christianity. But the Jesuit missionaries he sent to carry out his plans found that Christianity had to compete for followers with Zen Buddhism and Shinto, thriving and subtle faiths.

In China the task set for Christianity was even more demanding, for there the missionaries had to absorb the complex interplay between Buddhist, Taoist and Confucian thought before they themselves were accepted as intellectually respectable. This contact with sophisticated China and Japan taught missionaries a totally unmedieval quality—compromise in religious matters. The letter of Christianity sometimes had to be sacrificed for the spirit. For example, the significance of the Crucifixion had to be muted because the Japanese were shocked by the idea that the Son of God could be subjected to what they regarded as torture.

To avoid misapprehension, the missionaries had to master Chinese and Japanese and then decide at what point it would be wiser to introduce Latin, Spanish or Portuguese terms rather than use an inexact local approximation for a difficult theological concept. In the late 16th Century, the Jesuits in China went so far as to adopt Chinese dress and manner: they deprecated their own importance, flattered others, and prostrated themselves when given an audience by a powerful mandarin. All this was conduct that would have seemed utterly unacceptable to Christian missionaries up to that time.

The long-term effect on Christianity in Europe of its contacts with other religions was of great importance, though it is difficult to define this impact with precision. It led to a more relaxed view of dogma, a concentration on the promise rather than on the law of Christianity. Slowly it was realized that all men, however remote or primitive, had a religious sense that led them to worship something outside themselves and their immediate environment. In extreme cases this growing tolerance of other beliefs led to the vague pantheism which was to become widespread in the 18th Century—the belief that God dwells in everything and every man, and that God has not declared Himself exclusively to any one nation or sect.

Gradually, then, there grew up a positive respect for certain aspects of the lives of exotic peoples. There was admiration for their avoidance of the large-scale wars that were ravaging Europe. There was envy of their ability to enjoy life without the conscience-searching that the battle between Protestantism and Catholicism had intensified in Europe. Some of this approbation was the product of a nostalgia for the imagined carelessness and in-

nocence of the Earthly Paradise and of the Golden Age of antiquity; but much of the regard was based on direct observation, as when Caminha contrasted the physical charms and innocence of a naked Brazilian girl with the vanity and lesser attractions of the overdressed women of fashion in Europe.

As Europeans studied a multitude of societies—some of which seemed to give little weight to law, property or kings but which appeared to be made up nevertheless of handsome, happy and free individuals—they began to reflect on the flaws in their own governments. The conclusions drawn from such analytical comparisons underlay the work of 18th Century political writers like Rousseau, who saw Europeans as born in the chains of a needlessly elaborate and unfair social structure. The political and religious effects of these anthropological studies by explorers and missionaries would be felt in Europe over a long period of time.

There were still other effects of exploration, however, that were of far greater immediate importance to contemporary Europeans. Chief among these were various new products. One such novelty, tobacco, would take an increasingly prominent role as a consolation and cushion against the shocks of everyday existence. First encountered by Columbus in the West Indies, tobacco was introduced into France, Spain and Portugal by the mid-16th Century. By the early 17th Century, there was already raging an intense controversy about the effects of smoking on health.

Coffee, brought from Egypt and Turkey early in the 17th Century, at first met with opposition because of its Mohammedan origin. Legend has it that it was only when Pope Clement VIII approved its use that it became accepted in Europe—among other things, this laid the groundwork for the proliferation of coffeehouses where so much political and religious discussion was carried on during the 17th and 18th Centuries. Tea from China and

EXOTIC DANCERS *on the island of Java, accompanied by an instrument made of sugar-cane stalks, delighted early Dutch explorers with their graceful, sensuous movements. Gradually Europeans came to admire such unspoiled and highly civilized aspects of "uncivilized" societies.*

cocoa from South America, two other beverages which were to establish themselves richly in European life and literature, also came into use as a result of 16th and 17th Century exploration.

Sugar, the product that did so much to encourage the taste for these new beverages and did as much as spices to make the Renaissance diet more palatable, was native to southern Europe. But it was not until it was taken to the West Indies and Brazil by the Spaniards and Portuguese that it flourished sufficiently to become readily available to the average household. For most 16th Century European tables it was in fact a new product, far outweighing in usefulness such other newly intro-

duced foods as bananas and turkeys. Only one other product of the New World, the potato, exceeded sugar in importance. Widely cultivated in South America, potatoes became a major source of food for Europeans.

Exploration's ultimate effect on the status of European nations far exceeded its influence on the way Europeans ate, drank and smoked. The most clear-cut case is that of Portugal, whose importance was directly due to her explorers and the commercial empire which was built around their landfalls. The rise, the growing exhaustion and the dwindling world of Portugal all followed from Henry the Navigator's determination to explore the West African coast. It is fitting that Portugal's greatest poet, Luis Vaz de Camões, should have devoted his highest talents to commemorating the deeds of Vasco da Gama and other Portuguese heroes in his epic poem *The Lusiads*, published in 1572.

Spain's history, too, would have been notably different during the 16th Century if she had not followed up her explorers' reconnaissance with systematic exploitation of their rich discoveries. On the other hand, it must be recognized that Spain's important role during that century was determined largely by her growing efficiency as a nation after the union brought about by the marriage of Ferdinand of Aragon and Isabella of Castile in 1469. When their grandson, Charles I of Spain (later, as Charles V, Holy Roman Emperor), inherited the crown, Spain began to make the mounting international commitments in Italy, North Africa, and above all, in Germany and the Low Countries which ensured her place in world history. The gold and silver of the Americas may not have dictated the direction of this international involvement, but they certainly determined its scope.

In other parts of Europe, the discoveries of new lands had varied effects. They increased the tendency for the Atlantic to gain as a trading area at the expense of the Mediterranean. Ports like Lisbon and Antwerp, which received and distributed imports from Asia and the Americas, boomed steadily through most of the 16th Century. Actually, the origin of this prosperity antedated the explorations: the end of the Hundred Years' War in 1453 and the Wars of the Roses in 1485 had resulted in increasing stability in the northern countries of Europe, accompanied by improved trade and profits.

The Mediterranean ports had been appalled by the Portuguese success in securing the spices and silks of the Indies. But after a generation of disrupted and reduced traffic, those ancient ports were able to recover their trading vitality. Venice, for instance, which might have been expected to suffer most from the bypassing of her overland spice trade routes, increased her overall prosperity during the rest of the 16th Century, though her rate of growth was slower than that of some of her Atlantic rivals, like Antwerp.

The part played in exploration by the German states, France and England during this period was vigorous but sporadic. Exploration's effect on the fortunes of these countries was slight in comparison with the internal developments that were going on at the same time. Lessons in seamanship useful in future wars were learned by France and England, and their national self-consciousness was enhanced by their explorers' achievements. German capital helped to back not only German expeditions to South America, but those of other nations as well.

It was not until the 17th Century that the English and the Dutch, who were late in starting, notably increased their European stature by long-distance trade and overseas settlement. From that time on, however, their fortunes were closely tied to the new lands beyond the horizon.

Genuine scientific exploration, with its accurate chronometers, its teams of experts, its floating laboratories, blossomed at the end of the 18th Century and reached full flower in the remarkable feats of explorers of the 19th and 20th Centuries. But it is even more remarkable that the task of the later expeditions has been largely to verify and elaborate on the stupendous achievements of the days of sail and scurvy. The explorers of the Renaissance, often poor, often undervalued in their own time, are commemorated in every modern atlas; they have an enduring monument in that most useful roll of honor, the geographical gazetteer, in whose pages are listed the thousands of places—many still bearing their discoverers' names—that first became known to Europe through the Renaissance journeys into the unknown.

MYSTERIOUS STRANGERS, *in a detail from a 16th Century Persian rug, approach land on a towering ship.*

THROUGH NATIVE EYES

When European adventurers and merchants came sailing unexpectedly into their lives, Asians, Africans and Americans had one reaction in common: these white men were the most unusual creatures they had ever seen. Beyond this, the attitudes of different "discovered" peoples toward their visitors ranged widely, from awe to outright terror, from amusement to disdain. Native artists reported these impressions with graphic candor in many forms: totems, tapestries, carvings, lacquered screens. From their work comes a fresh and often revealing record of the appearance, manners and mores of the explorers who arrived on their shores.

THE CRITICAL JAPANESE

Portuguese traders, seen here astride their fine, handsome horses in a detail from a painted paper screen, were considered neither refined nor handsome by their Japanese hosts, who found Westerners incredibly gross: their noses were too large, their mustaches too fierce, their legs too long. They also wore

billowing pantaloons, which the Japanese delighted to exaggerate in their paintings. Still, these physical features might have been acceptable if the Europeans had balanced them with decent manners. But the Japanese considered most foreigners barbarously crude and chose to tolerate their intrusive presence only a short while. In 1638, less than a hundred years after the first Westerners arrived, the ruling shogun and his ministers expelled all but a few favored Dutch. First, however, they were careful to breed Japan's undersized Mongolian ponies to the stronger, fleeter Arabian horses of the interlopers.

AN AFRICAN AWE OF ARMAMENT

To the skilled artists of the Nigerian kingdom of Benin, the Europeans' most impressive aspect—even more extraordinary
than their skin color—was their weaponry.
African bronze and ivory work presented
European crossbows, matchlocks, swords
and daggers in precise detail, while the
faces of the men carrying them *(right)* often appeared to be little more than masks.
There may be a simple explanation for the
meticulous attention that African craftsmen gave firearms. Many primitive peoples believed that by making a model of
an object, one could possess its magic—
and 16th Century Africans must have
wanted desperately to exorcise the special
and terrible magic of European guns.

Whatever the reasoning behind these
graphic carvings, the ancient skill that
produced them impressed the Portuguese.
They began to instruct native artists in
making and decorating such European ar-
ticles as spoons and saltcellars, which
were later enjoyed in Portugal as samples of the riches of the new-found world.

A EUROPEAN SOLDIER *appears in a Benin bronze
plaque (right) with a carefully detailed crossbow in one hand and its ammunition in the other. In the African ivory carving at far right, a
knight and his attendant decorating a cylindri-
cal saltcellar are armed with swords and spears.*

FROM THE AZTECS, A RECORD
OF CRUEL DECEPTION

The Aztecs of Mexico recorded their devastating struggle with the conquistadors in transcribed narratives and vivid picture-writing, both preserved on scrolls called codices. According to codex writers, Aztec terror of the Spanish began the instant King Montezuma received a message that light-skinned men were arriving on "towers or small

A PIKE-BEARING SPANIARD *faces an Aztec warrior before the Great Temple in Tenochtitlán, the Mexican capital. Behind them, another Aztec beats a ceremonial drum used during human sacrifices.*

A MASSACRE OF CELEBRANTS *takes place during an Aztec festival. The Spaniards deceitfully struck the unarmed native warriors "when the dance was loveliest and when song was linked to song."*

mountains floating on the waves of the sea." His wizards had predicted catastrophe for his empire, and Montezuma feared it was to come with the advent of these men. Ruler of a pious people, he tried to appease the strangers by sprinkling their food with the fresh, bright blood of human sacrifice intended for the gods. To his and his priests' confusion, however, the Spanish "closed their eyes and shook their heads in abhorrence" at the sight.

Shortly after, the Aztecs learned to their own shock that not all bloodshed distressed the white man. The Spanish conquest of Mexico was accompanied by the ruthless slaughter of the Aztecs; the codices about this period read like classical tragedies.

A SHARP BUT GENTLE VIEW FROM INDIA

India, of all "discovered" countries, was probably the least overwhelmed by the onslaught of Europeans. Accustomed for centuries to foreign visitors —and invaders—from across the Arabian Sea or through the Himalayan passes, India also had the advantage of a religious tradition that could accept the One God theme in any variation a missionary might suggest. In 1578, the Mogul Emperor Akbar opened his court to discussions with Parsi priests,

Jain saints and Hindu wise men as well as orthodox Moslems; the Christian Jesuits who arrived with the explorers were simply welcomed into his circle. Indian artists showed similar aplomb. If at first they focused on the newcomers' unusual costumes and such strange mannerisms as holding lace handkerchiefs, later they began to paint individual Portuguese and Englishmen with a sharpness European artists might well have admired.

AN ENGLISH SETTLER *(right), smoking a hookah and attended by Indian servants, takes his ease amid Oriental cushions. He is probably Dr. William Fullarton, a Scottish surgeon with the East India Company.*

ELEGANT TRAVELER *walks through Indian landscape with distinctly foreign vigor. Such men were welcome at court: the Emperor "associated with the good of every race" and was curious about Westerners.*

NO LONGER FOREIGN, *Europeans at a banquet appear almost Oriental on a 17th Century bedspread from Golconda in central India. Even their clothe*

em to fall in Eastern folds. As Westerners became familiar figures all over the world, their alien qualities slowly began to fade from native art.

GREAT AGES OF WORLD CIVILIZATION

The chart below shows the approximate duration of the Age of Exploration in relation to the important cultural periods of the Western world, the central Mediterranean and African regions, and the East. It is excerpted from a more comprehensive world chronology which appears in the introductory booklet to the Great Ages of Man series.

On the following two pages there appears a chronological table of some of the more important events that took place throughout the world during the epoch covered by this book.

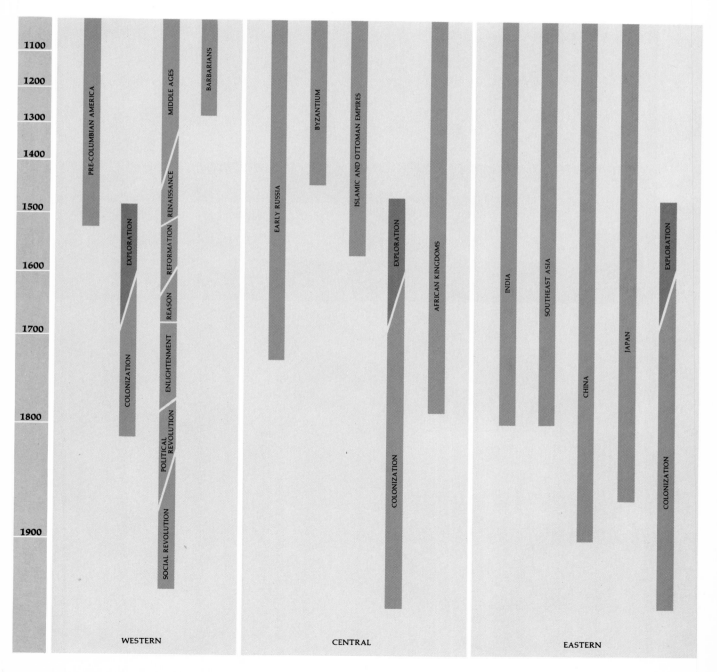

WESTERN	CENTRAL	EASTERN

CHRONOLOGY: A listing of significant events during the Age of Exploration

Voyages and Discoveries

1415 Portugal captures Ceuta in Morocco, beginning overseas expansion
1418 Portuguese land in the Madeira Islands

1434 Africa's Cape Bojador, the southern limit of the known world, is rounded
1439 Portuguese colonize the Azores
1441 Slave trade begins in Africa's Rio do Ouro region
1444 Portuguese reach the mouth of the Senegal River in Africa

1456 Cadamosto discovers the Cape Verde Islands for Portugal
1460 Portuguese reach Sierra Leone

1477 The first printed edition of Ptolemy's *Geography* appears

1483 Diogo Cão explores the Congo River

1488 Bartolomeu Dias rounds the Cape of Good Hope
1492 Columbus discovers the Bahama Islands and Cuba and claims them for Spain (First Voyage)
1493 Columbus sights Puerto Rico, Jamaica (Second Voyage)
1494 Treaty of Tordesillas divides the undiscovered world between Spain and Portugal
1497 John Cabot explores the North American coast for England
1498 Vasco da Gama reaches India, opening an all-sea route for Portugal
1498 Columbus sights the South American coast (Third Voyage)
1500 Cabral claims Brazil for Portugal

1502 Columbus explores the Central American coast (Fourth Voyage)
1507 Martin Waldseemüller's world map labels the new southern continent "America"

1509 Portuguese overcome Moslem sea power at the Battle of Diu
1510 Albuquerque takes the Indian city of Goa for Portugal
1511 Albuquerque occupies Malacca, giving Portugal a base in the Indies
1513 Portuguese ships reach China and the Moluccas
1513 Balboa crosses the Isthmus of Panama, sights the Pacific Ocean

Politics and Culture

1405 Chinese Ming Dynasty begins sending fleets to India, Persia, Africa on political and trade mission

1427 Thomas à Kempis writes *Imitation of Christ*
1434 The Medici come to power in Florence

1440 Lorenzo Valla proves Donation of Constantine a forgery, undermining temporal authority of the papacy

1450 West African kingdom of Benin flourishes; Aztecs dominate Mexico
1453 Turks conquer Constantinople; Byzantine refugees bring priceless classical manuscripts to the West
1453 End of 100 Years' War between England and France
1454 Gutenberg produces the first printed Bible
1455 Wars of the Roses divide England for 30 years

1469 Lorenzo de' Medici heads Florentine state
1469 Marriage of Ferdinand and Isabella unifies Spain
1471 Sixtus IV becomes Pope, strengthens the Papal States

1478 Spanish Inquisition begins
1479 Turks defeat Venice after a 16-year war and impose payment for trading privileges
1480 Ivan III frees duchy of Moscow from Tatar rule

1485 Henry VII founds Tudor dynasty, ending civil war in England

1492 Spanish conquer Moorish kingdom of Granada, expel Moors and Jews

1494 Charles VIII of France invades Italy, beginning 65 years of French and Spanish wars there
1495 Leonardo da Vinci paints *The Last Supper*

1498 Savonarola is burned at the stake in Florence for heresy

1508 Michelangelo begins to paint the Sistine Chapel ceiling
1509 Erasmus publishes *Praise of Folly*

1513 Machiavelli publishes *The Prince*
1516 Thomas More publishes *Utopia*

1519 Habsburg Charles I of Spain is elected Holy Roman Emperor Charles V

1425

1450

1475

1500

RENAISSANCE

GREAT DISCOVERIES

1524 The Peasants' War begins to ravage Germany
1526 Mogul (Mongol) dynasty is founded in India
1528 Castiglione publishes *The Courtier*
1529 Turks unsuccessfully besiege Vienna

1533 Rabelais begins publishing his comic masterpiece *Gargantua and Pantagruel*
1534 Henry VIII of England breaks with Rome and founds the Anglican Church
1536 John Calvin publishes *Institutes of the Christian Religion*

1540 Society of Jesus (Jesuits) is founded, revitalizing Catholicism
1541 Calvin rules Geneva as a theocracy
1542 Congregation of the Inquisition is established in Rome to root out heretics
1543 Copernicus publishes his *Revolutions of the Celestial Orbs*

1547 Ivan IV adopts the title of Czar of Russia

1555 Peace of Augsburg divides Germany between Lutheran and Catholic princes
1556 Holy Roman Emperor Charles V abdicates; Habsburg domains are divided
1556 Reign of Philip II begins Spain's "century of gold"
1558 Elizabeth I succeeds to the throne in England
1562 France enters 36 years of religious and civil wars
1568 The Netherlands revolt against Spanish rule

1571 Spanish and Venetian navies defeat Turks at Lepanto
1572 Protestant Huguenot population in France is massacred
1572 Camões finishes *The Lusiads*, the Portuguese national epic
1580 Portugal is incorporated into the Spanish empire
1580 Montaigne publishes his *Essays* on various forms of government
1588 The Spanish Armada is routed by the English fleet and North Sea storms
1589 Henry IV founds Bourbon dynasty in France, ending religious wars

1597 Japanese expel Western missionaries

1605 Cervantes begins publishing *Don Quixote*

1611 Shakespeare presents *The Tempest*
1611 King James Bible is published
1613 Romanov dynasty increases Russian power

1618 Thirty Years' War begins in Germany

REFORMATION

1525

RISE OF NATIONALISM

1550

1575

1600

ERA OF CONSOLIDATION

SETTLEMENTS AND COMMERCE

1524 Verrazano explores the mouth of the Hudson for France

1532 Pizarro conquers the Inca empire

1535 Cartier explores the St. Lawrence River
1535 Spanish establish Lima in Peru
1539 De Soto explores what is now the southeastern United States
1541 Coronado explores the territory west of the Mississippi

1549 Portuguese reach Kagoshima in Japan
1553 Sir Hugh Willoughby perishes while searching for a northeast passage to China

1569 Gerhardus Mercator publishes a world map using his famous projection

1571 Spaniards found Manila in the Philippines

1580 Sir Francis Drake completes his circumnavigation of the globe, landing en route near San Francisco

1589 Hakluyt publishes *The Principal Navigations of the English Nation*
1595 Dutch explore the East Indies

1600 English East India Company is chartered
1602 Dutch East India Company is chartered

1606 Queiros discovers the northern New Hebrides Islands
1606 Janszoon sights the coast of Australia
1606 Torres sails south around New Guinea
1607 English settle in Jamestown and prosper by raising tobacco
1608 Champlain founds a French colony at Quebec
1610 Henry Hudson explores Hudson Bay

1615 Dutch settle Manhattan Island as a fur-trading post

1620 English Pilgrims land at Plymouth Bay

BIBLIOGRAPHY

These books were selected during the preparation of the volume for their interest and authority, and for their usefulness to readers seeking additional information on specific points.

An asterisk (*) marks works available in both hard-cover and paperback editions; a dagger (†) indicates availability only in paperback.

GENERAL

Baker, J.N.L., *A History of Geographical Discovery and Exploration*. George G. Harrap, 1948.

Baudet, Henri, *Paradise on Earth*. Yale University Press, 1965.

Bettex, Albert, *The Discovery of the World*. Simon and Schuster, 1960.

Clark, William R., *Explorers of the World*. Natural History Press, 1964.

Hakluyt, Richard, ed., *Voyages* (8 vols.). Dutton, 1962.

Leithäuser, Joachim G., *Worlds Beyond The Horizon*. Alfred A. Knopf, 1955.

Lips, Julius E., *The Savage Hits Back*. Yale University Press, 1937.

Nowell, Charles E., *A History of Portugal*. D. Van Nostrand, 1952.

*Parry, J. H., *The Age of Reconnaissance*. World Publishing Company, 1963.

*Penrose, Boies, *Travel and Discovery in the Renaissance 1420-1620*. Harvard University Press, 1952.

Robertson, James A., transl. and ed., *Magellan's Voyage Around the World—by Antonio Pigafetta* (3 vols.). Arthur H. Clark, 1906.

Rugoff, Milton, ed., *The Great Travelers* (2 vols.). Simon and Schuster, 1960.

Sanceau, Elaine, *Henry the Navigator*. Norton, 1947.

Washburn, W. E., "The Meaning of 'Discovery' in the 15th and 16th Centuries," *American Historical Review*, October 1962.

Weinstock, Herbert, transl. and ed., *Francesco Carletti: My Voyage around the World*. Random House, 1964.

Zumthor, Paul, *Daily Life in Rembrandt's Holland*. Macmillan, 1963.

SHIPS, NAVIGATION AND CARTOGRAPHY

Chatterton, E. Keble, *Ships and Ways of Other Days*. J. B. Lippincott, 1913.

Cipolla, Carlo M., *Guns and Sails in the Early Phase of European Expansion, 1400-1700*. Collins, 1965.

Crone, Gerald R., *Maps and Their Makers*. Hillary House, 1953.

Landström, Björn, *The Ship: An Illustrated History*. Doubleday, 1961.

Skelton, R. A., *Explorers' Maps*. Frederick A. Praeger, 1958.

Taylor, E.G.R., *The Haven-Finding Art*. Abelard-Schuman, 1957.

Waters, David Watkins, *The Art of Navigation in England in Elizabethan and Early Stuart Times*. Yale University Press, 1958.

AFRICA AND THE EAST

Blake, John W., transl. and ed., *Europeans in West Africa 1450-1560* (2 vols.). Hakluyt Society, 1942.

Boxer, Charles R., ed., *South China in the Sixteenth Century*. Hakluyt Society, 1953.

Boxer, Charles R., *The Christian Century in Japan 1549-1650*. University of California Press, 1951.

Boxer, Charles R., *The Dutch Seaborne Empire, 1600-1800*. Alfred A. Knopf, 1965.

Crone, Gerald R., transl. and ed., *The Voyages of Cadamosto*. Hakluyt Society, 1937.

Edwardes, Michael, *A History of India*. Farrar, Straus and Cudahy, 1961.

Gallagher, Louis J., and S. J. Gallagher, transl., *China in the Sixteenth Century: The Journals of Matthew Ricci, 1583-1610*. Random House, 1953.

Greenlee, W. B., transl. and ed., *The Voyage of Pedro Alvares Cabral to Brazil and India*. Hakluyt Society, 1938.

Hart, Henry H., *Sea Road to the Indies*. Macmillan, 1950.

Jones, John W., transl., *The Travels of Ludovico di Varthema*. Hakluyt Society, 1863.

Lach, Donald F., *Asia in the Making of Europe* (2 vols.). University of Chicago Press, 1965.

Ley, Charles D., ed., *Portuguese Voyages 1498-1663*. Dutton, 1960.

*Mandeville, John, *The Travels of Sir John Mandeville*. Dover, 1964.

Prestage, Edgar, *The Portuguese Pioneers*. A. & C. Black, 1933.

Ravenstein, E. G., transl. and ed., *A Journal of the First Voyage of Vasco da Gama, 1497-1499*. Hakluyt Society, 1898.

Rogers, Francis M., *The Quest for Eastern Christians*. University of Minnesota Press, 1962.

Sansom, George, *A History of Japan* (3 vols.). Stanford University Press, 1958-1963.

Sansom, G. B., *The Western World and Japan*. Alfred A. Knopf, 1950.

Smith, Bradley, *Japan: A History in Art*. Simon and Schuster, 1964.

THE NEW WORLD

Bandelier, A. F., *The Gilded Man*. Rio Grande Press, 1962.

Biggar, H. P., transl. and ed., *The Voyages of Jacques Cartier*. Public Archives of Canada, 1924.

*Brebner, John Bartlet, *The Explorers of North America 1492-1806*. Peter Smith, 1955.

Collinson, Richard, *The Three Voyages of Martin Frobisher*. Hakluyt Society, undated.

Crow, John A., *The Epic of Latin America*. Doubleday, 1946.

Haskins, Caryl P., *The Amazon*. Doubleday, 1943.

Hoffman, Bernard G., *Cabot to Cartier*. University of Toronto Press, 1961.

*Kirkpatrick, F. A., *The Spanish Conquistadores*. Peter Smith, 1962.

Leon-Portilla, Miguel, ed., *The Broken Spears; The Aztec Account of the Conquest of Mexico*. Beacon, 1962.

Lorant, Stefan, ed., *The New World: The First Pictures of America*. Duell, Sloan and Pearce, 1965.

† Major, R. H., transl. and ed., *Christopher Columbus: Four Voyages to the New World*. Corinth Books, 1961.

Means, Philip A., *The Spanish Main*. Gordian, 1965.

Medina, Jose Toribio, *The Discovery of the Amazon*. American Geographical Society, 1934.

Millar, George, *A Crossbowman's Story of the First Exploration of the Amazon*. Alfred A. Knopf, 1955.

Morison, Samuel Eliot, *Admiral of the Ocean Sea*. Little, Brown, 1942.

Morison, Samuel Eliot, transl. and ed., *Journals and Other Documents on the Life and Voyages of Christopher Columbus*. Heritage Press, 1963.

Oleson, Tryggvi J., *Early Voyages and Northern Approaches*. McClelland and Stewart, 1963.

Pohl, Frederick J., *Amerigo Vespucci, Pilot Major*. Columbia University Press, 1944.

Schulthess, Emil, *The Amazon*. Simon and Schuster, 1962.

Swan, Michael, *The Marches of El Dorado*. Beacon Press, 1959.

Wallace, Willard M., *Sir Walter Raleigh*. Princeton University Press, 1959.

THE SEARCH FOR NORTHERN PASSAGES

Dodge, Ernest S., *Northwest by Sea*. Oxford University Press, 1961.

Kirwan, L. P., *A History of Polar Exploration*. Norton, 1959.

Markham, Clements R., *A Life of John Davis, the Navigator*. Dodd, Mead, 1889.

THE PACIFIC AND TERRA AUSTRALIS

Beaglehole, J. C., ed., *The Endeavour Journal of Joseph Banks, 1768-1771* (2 vols.). Angus & Robertson, 1962.

Beaglehole, J. C., *The Exploration of the Pacific*. Adam & Charles Black, 1934.

Beaglehole, J. C., ed., *The Journals of Captain James Cook* (Vols. I and II). Cambridge University Press, 1961.

Cameron, Roderick W., *The Golden Haze: with Captain Cook in the South Pacific*. World Publishing Company, 1964.

Carrington, Hugh, ed., *The Discovery of Tahiti*. Cambridge University Press, 1948.

Clark, C.M.H., *A History of Australia* (Vol. 1). Cambridge University Press, 1962.

Cook, James, and James King, *A Voyage to the Pacific Ocean*. London, 1784.

Dunmore, John, *French Explorers in the Pacific*. Oxford University Press, 1965.

Gwyther, John, *Captain Cook and the South Pacific*. Houghton Mifflin, 1954.

Markham, Clements, transl. and ed., *The Voyages of Pedro Fernandez de Quiros* (2 vols.). Hakluyt Society, 1904.

Moorehead, Alan, *The Fatal Impact*. Hamish Hamilton, 1966.

Price, A. Grenfell, ed., *The Explorations of Captain James Cook*. Heritage Press, undated.

Riesenberg, Felix, *The Pacific Ocean*. Whittlesey House, 1940.

Smith, Bernard, *European Vision and the South Pacific, 1768-1850*. Oxford University Press, 1960.

Wallis, Helen, ed., *Carteret's Voyage Round the World, 1766-1769* (2 vols.). Cambridge University Press, 1965.

Warner, Oliver, *Captain Cook and the South Pacific*. American Heritage, 1963.

Williamson, James A., *Cook and the Opening of the Pacific*. Macmillan, 1948.

*Williamson, James A., *The Age of Drake*. Barnes and Noble, 1960.

ART INFORMATION AND PICTURE CREDITS

The sources for the illustrations in this book are set forth below. Descriptive notes on the works of art are included. Credits for pictures positioned from left to right are separated by semicolons, from top to bottom by dashes. Photographers' names which follow a descriptive note appear in parentheses. Abbreviations include "c." for century and "ca." for circa.

Cover—The Cape of Good Hope and Terra Australis, illumination from *Cosmographie universelle selon les navigateurs anciens que modernes* by Guillaume le Testu, 1555, Ministère des Armées, Paris (Eric Schaal).

CHAPTER 1: 10—*Storm at Sea* by Pieter Brueghel the Elder, oil on wood, ca. 1568, Kunsthistorisches Museum, Vienna (Erich Lessing from Magnum). 12-13—Christopher Colum-

bus on the island of Hispaniola. From *Peregrinationes in Indiam Orientalem et Occidentalem*, Part IV, by Theodor de Bry, 1594. 15—Facsimile map of Scandinavia and North Atlantic, Olaus Magnus, woodcut, 1539, Venice, British Museum, London (John R. Freeman). 18—Constellation of Perseus with the Head of Medusa from the *Book of the Fixed Stars* by 'Abd al-Raham al-Sufi, inks on paper, early 15th c., The Metropolitan Museum of Art, New York, Rogers Fund (Albert Fenn). 21—Photograph by Fritz Goro. 22—Photograph by Leonard McCombe. 23—Photograph by Fritz Goro. 24-25—Photograph from Freelance Photographers Guild. 26-27—Photographs by Ernst Haas from Magnum. 28-29—Photograph by Leonard McCombe.

CHAPTER 2: 30—The City of Macao from *India Orientalis*, Part VIII, by Theodor de Bry, 1598 Edition, Rare Book Division, New York Public Library. 33—Monsters of Siberia, illumination from *Livre des Merveilles*, 1375, Bibliothèque Nationale, Paris. 37—Portrait of Vasco da Gama from a Portuguese manuscript, after 1524, Cabinet des Manuscrits, Bibliothèque Nationale, Paris (Anthony Linck). 39—*Syndics of the Guild of St. Luke at Haarlem*, by Jan de Bray, oil on canvas, 1675, Rijksmuseum, Amsterdam. 40-41—*The Return of the Dutch Fleet from Brazil* by Hendrik Cornelius Vroom, oil on canvas, 17th c., Rijksmuseum, Amsterdam. 42-43—*Still-Life with Lobster and Turkey* by Abraham van Beyeren, oil on canvas, 1660, courtesy The Ashmolean Museum, Oxford; *Merry Company* by Jan Steen, oil on canvas, ca. 1665, Mauritshuis, The Hague (Eddy van der Veen). 44-45—*The Linen Cupboard* by Pieter de Hooch, oil on canvas, 1663, Rijksmuseum, Amsterdam; *A Young Woman in a Red Jacket Feeding a Parrot* by Frans van Mieris, oil on canvas, 1663, courtesy the Trustees of the National Gallery, London (Derek Bayes)—*Still-Life with a Pewter Flagon and Two Ming Bowls* by Jan Treck, oil on canvas, 1649, courtesy the Trustees of the National Gallery, London (Derek Bayes). 46-47—*Interior of an Art Gallery*, Flemish School, oil on canvas, 17th c., courtesy the Trustees of the National Gallery, London. 48-49—*The Return of the East Indian Company to Batavia* by Albert Cuyp, oil on canvas, 17th c., Rijksmuseum, Amsterdam.

CHAPTER 3: 50—*Christopher Columbus* attributed to Ridolfo del Ghirlandaio, oil on wood, ca. 1525, Museo Civico Navale di Genova-Pegli (Aldo Durazzi). 61—*The Geographer* by Vermeer van Delft, oil on canvas, ca. 1673, Stadelsches Kunstinstitut, Frankfurt am Main (Joachim Blauel). 62-63—World map according to Ptolemy from the *Ulm Atlas* of 1482, British Museum, London (Derek Bayes); world map by Henricius Martellus Germanus, 1489, color on vellum, British Museum, London—celestial globe upheld by Atlas, 1st-2nd c., from a prototype of the Hellenistic Age, marble, Museo Nazionale, Naples (Emmett Bright). 64-65—*Cantino Planisphere*, Portuguese, color on parchment, ca. 1502, Biblioteca Estense Universitaria, Modena (David Lees). 66-67—Celestial map by Albrecht Dürer, woodcut, 1515, The Metropolitan Museum of Art, New York, Dick Fund (Albert Fenn). 68-69—*Salviati Planisphere*, Spanish, colors on parchment, 1525-1530, Biblioteca Medicea-Laurenziana, Florence (Guido Sansoni)—illumination from *Cosmographie* by Jacques Devault, 1583, Bibliothèque Nationale, Paris. 70-71—World Map by Johann Blaeu, engraving, 1641, British Museum, London (Derek Bayes).

CHAPTER 4: 72—Arab and European astrolabes, brass and gilt brass, 14th-16th centuries, courtesy Museum of the History of Science, Oxford (Dr. H. Zinram). 74—Diagram by John Condon. 77—*Carte Pisane*, ink on parchment, ca. 1275, Bibliothèque Nationale, Paris. 78—*The Figure of the Quadrant*, from Samuel Storing's *Mariner's Magazine*, 1663, National Maritime Museum, Greenwich, England—sextant, courtesy New York Nautical Instrument and Service Corp. (Ted Russell). 81—Compass card from John Davis' *Seamen's Secrets*, 1596, British Museum, London (John R. Freeman). 82—*Carrack in the Harbor of Mothoni* by Erhard Reuwich, woodcut, 1486, from *Bernhard von Breydenbach: The Crusades to Jerusalem*, Kunstbibliothek der Staatlichen Museen Berlin (Robert Lackenbach from Black Star). 85-93—Drawings by Victor Lazzaro in consultation with William Baker, naval architect, Curator, Hart Nautical Museum, Massachusetts Institute of Technology, Cambridge. 86-87—From drawings by Björn Landström in his *The Ship: An Illustrated History*, Doubleday, 1961.

CHAPTER 5: 94—Chinese Scene from *India Orientalis*, Part II, by Theodor de Bry, 1598 edition, Rare Book Division, New York Public Library. 100—Cathedral of the Archangel Michael, designed by Alevisio Novyi, brick and white stone, begun 1505, Moscow (Pierre Boulat). 103—Marco Polo before the Khan in Cathay, illumination from *Marco Polo, Les Livres du Granut Caam*, ca. 1400, Bodleian Library, Oxford. 105—South America, engraved from a map by Diego Gutiérrez, 1562, British Museum, London (R. B. Fleming). 106-115—Photographs by Emil Schulthess from Black Star.

CHAPTER 6: 116—Barents' men leaving ice-bound ship from *India Orientalis*, Part III, by Theodor de Bry, after Gerrit de Veer, 1598 edition, Rare Book Division, New York Public Library (Robert Kafka). 119—Polar map by John Dee, ink on vellum, 1582, Free Public Library, Philadelphia (Fernand Bourges). 122—*Eskimo Woman and Baby* by John White, watercolor, 1577, British Museum, London (Lee Boltin). 125—Barents expedition's winter quarters in the Arctic by Theodor de Bry, after Gerrit de Veer, *India*

Orientalis, Part III, 1598 edition, Rare Book Division, New York Public Library (Robert Kafka). 127-135—Watercolors by John White, 1577-1590, British Museum, London (Lee Boltin).

CHAPTER 7: 136—*Captain Cook* by Nathaniel Dance, oil on canvas, 1776, courtesy the National Maritime Museum, Greenwich (Lee Boltin). 144—Figure, probably an upright architectural element from a house, Maori, New Zealand, wood, probably 18th c., courtesy The Museum of Primitive Art, New York. 147—H.M.S. *Endeavour* hull, pencil drawing, British Museum, London. 148—*Endeavour*'s small boats, drawing by A. Buchan, British Museum, London—Indian village, Tierra del Fuego, engraving by S. Parkinson, from *A Journal of a Voyage to the South Seas, in His Majesty's Ship, The Endeavour*, London, 1773, Rare Book Division, New York Public Library. 149—Inhabitants of Tierra del Fuego in their huts, watercolor by A. Buchan, British Museum, London—tropic bird, watercolor by S. Parkinson, The Natural History Museum, London (Lee Boltin). 150—Tahitian heads, engraving from a drawing by S. Parkinson, National Maritime Museum, Greenwich (Lee Boltin)—Tahitian chief's house, engraving from a drawing by S. Parkinson, British Museum, London (Lee Boltin). 151—Instruments and utensils of Tahitians, engraving from a drawing by S. H. Grimm, National Maritime Museum, Greenwich (Lee Boltin)—breadfruit plant of Tahiti, watercolor by S. Parkinson, The Natural History Museum, London (Derek Bayes). 152—Maori tattoo design, pencil drawing by S. Parkinson, British Museum, London—New Zealand Maori warriors, pen and ink and wash by S. Parkinson, British Museum, London. 153—The *Endeavour* beached, engraving, National Maritime Museum, Greenwich (Lee Boltin)—kangaroo, engraving from S. Parkinson sketch, National Maritime Museum, Greenwich (Lee Boltin). 154—Bearded penguin, watercolor by George Forster, The Natural History Museum, London (Lee Boltin)—*Endeavour*'s seamen gather ice for drinking water, engraving by B. T. Pouncy from drawing by W. Hodges, British Museum, London. 155—Fish of New Zealand, watercolor by George Forster, The Natural History Museum, London (Lee Boltin)—landing at Tanna, New Hebrides, engraved from a painting by W. Hodges, National Maritime Museum, Greenwich (Lee Boltin). 156-157—Boxing match at Hapaee in the Friendly Islands, engraved from a drawing by J. Webber, British Museum, London; Tahitian ladies dancing, watercolor by John Webber, British Museum, London; Cook watching human sacrifice, watercolor by John Webber, British Museum, London. 158—Girl from Prince William Sound, Vancouver, engraving from a drawing by J. Webber, British Museum, London—hunting sea horses off Alaska, engraving from a drawing by J. Webber, National Maritime Museum, Greenwich (Lee Boltin)—house interior, Unalaska, engraving from a drawing by J. Webber, National Maritime Museum, Greenwich (Lee Boltin). 159—Captain Cook killed by Hawaiians, engraving from a drawing by J. Webber, in the *Atlas of Cook's Third Voyage*, National Maritime Museum, London (Lee Boltin).

CHAPTER 8: 160—Christian and Native Wives in Portuguese India (Goa) from *Album of Illustrations Showing Uses and Customs of the people of Africa and Asia*, Portuguese, watercolor, 1628, Biblioteca Casanatense, Rome (Vivarelli). 162—Ornament, Chimú, pre-Inca, gold, ca. 1000, courtesy Museo Nacional de Arqueologia, Rafael Hoyle, Lima, Peru (Peter Anderson from Black Star). 165—*Hippopotamus*, from a bound volume of watercolors, Austrian, late 16th c. Codex S.n. 2647, Osterreichische Nationalbibliothek, Vienna. 166—*La Chine Illustrée* by Athanasium Kircher, Amsterdam, 1670, New York Public Library (Robert Kafka). 169—Javanese Dancers from *India Orientalis* by Theodor de Bry, 1598 edition, Rare Book Division, New York Public Library. 171—Detail from a Persian carpet, Isphahan, wool, 16th c., Musée des Tissus, Lyon (Andre Gamet-Rapho from Rapho Guillumette). 172-173—Horse race, detail from a Japanese southern barbarian screen, colors on paper, early 17th c., Suntory Gallery, Tokyo (T. Tanuma). 174-175—Portuguese Soldier with crossbow from Benin, West Africa, bronze, later 16th c., British Museum, London (Werner Forman); Afro-Portuguese container, may have been made by African craftsmen in Portugal, ivory, late 16th c., British Museum, London (Werner Forman). 176-177—Massacre of the Aztecs by Spanish warriors at the feast of Toxcatl, color lithograph after original illustrations in the Codex of Diego de Duran entitled *A History of the Indies and of New Spain*, ca. 1588, Library of Congress, courtesy American Heritage Publishing Co., Inc.; Spanish warrior arriving before the Great Temple, from an Aztec history, miniature painting, 1576, British Museum, London (John R. Freeman). 178—English Traveler in India, miniature painting, ca. 1600, Mogul India, Victoria & Albert Museum, London (A. C. Cooper, Ltd.). 179—Probably a portrait of Dr. William Fullerton in Bengal, India, by Dip Chand, miniature painting, 1760, Victoria & Albert Museum, London, courtesy American Heritage Publishing Co., Inc. 180-181—Printed cotton bedspread from Golconda, India, 17th c., Victoria & Albert Museum, London (A. C. Cooper, Ltd.).

ACKNOWLEDGMENTS

The editors of this book are particularly indebted to Robin W. Winks, Associate Professor of History, Yale University; Harry Bernstein, Professor of History, Brooklyn College, City University of New York; William Baker, Curator of The Hart Nautical Museum, Massachusetts Institute of Technology; Frederick J. Dockstader, Director of The Museum of the American Indian, New York; Edouard Stackpole, Curator of Mystic Seaport Marine Historical Association; Lewis Stark, Chief of Rare Book Division, New York Public Library; Maud Cole, Assistant Chief of Rare Book Division, New York Public Library; Mary F.A. Myers, Metropolitan Museum of Art, New York; Robert Carneiro, Associate Curator of South American Ethnology, American Museum of Natural History, New York; John Maass, Visual Presentation Director of the City of Philadelphia; Nicola Mazzaracchio, Director, and Ermenegildo Prosperi, Direzione Generale delle Accademie e Biblioteche, Rome; Carla Mancini, Biblioteca Nazionale, Rome; Marcella Mariani, Director, and Laura Olivieri, Biblioteca Casanatense, Rome; Irma Merolle-Tondi, Director of Biblioteca Medicea-Laurenziana, Florence; Pietro Puliatti of Biblioteca Estense, Modena; Tullia Gasparrini Leporace, Director of Biblioteca Marciana, Venice; Giovanni Annibaldi, Director of Museo Nazionale, Ancona; Ferdinando Rodriguez, Director of Biblioteca Universitaria, Bologna; Romeo Parisotto, Ente Provinciale per il Turismo, Vicenza; Caterina Marcenaro, Director, and Maria Campelli, Ufficio Belle Arti, Genoa; Laura Secchi, Director of Museo Navale Genoa-Pegli; Luigi Marchini, Director, and Rosella Piatti, Biblioteca Civica Berio, Genoa; Ettore Zanzarotto, Director of Istituto Internazionale delle Comunicazioni, Genoa; Emil Kümmerer, Universitätsbibliothek, Tübingen; Helmut Grötzsch, Staatlicher Mathematisch-Physikalischer Salon, Dresden; Deutsches Museum, Munich; Thüringische Landesbibliothek, Weimar; Kupferstichkabinet, Staatliche Museum zu Berlin; Kunstgewerbemuseum, Berlin; Margarethe Feldhaus, Heidelberg; Stadtbibliothek, Ulm; Violetta Becker-Donner, Museum für Völkerkunde, Vienna; Hans Paur, Bildarchiv der National Bibliothek, Vienna; Erwin M. Auer, Director of Kunsthistorisches Museum, Vienna; G. Naish, National Maritime Museum, Greenwich; British Museum, London; The Natural History Museum, London; Science Museum, London; National Gallery, London; Indian Section of the Victoria and Albert Museum, London; Chester Beatty Library, Dublin; Bodleian Library, Oxford; Marguerite Deneck, Assistant Curator, Musée Guimet; Edmond Pognon, Curator, and Monique de la Roncierre, Roger Hervé and Lucie LaGarde, Département des Cartes et Plans, Bibliothèque Nationale, Paris.

INDEX

This symbol in front of a page number indicates a photograph or painting of the subject mentioned.

A

Acapulco, Mexico, 137
Aden, *map* 37
Aeterni regis, papal bull, *map* 57
Afghanistan, exploration of, 102
Africa: on Cantino chart, *map* 64-65; East, indigenous sailing craft, 14; European medieval ideas of, 31-32, 33; European settlement, 34; first circumnavigation of, 34-35, *map* 37; mapping of east coast, *map* 64-65, *map* 69, 95; mapping of west coast, *map* 63-65; missionaries in, 167; native attitudes toward Europeans, 35, 83, 174; penetration of interior, 163; Portuguese exploration of coast, of, 18, 32, 33-35, 36, *map* 37, 38, 51; Portuguese trading posts, 102; in Ptolemy's world, *map* 62; sculpture, *174-175; Spanish exploration of west coast of, 18, 34; trade with, 32, 33-34, 53
Agra, India, 102
Ailly, Pierre d', 52
Akbar, Mogul Emperor, 179
Alaska, Cook in, 156, *158
Albuquerque, Afonso de, 103
Aleutian Islands, Cook in, *158
Alexander VI, Pope, 57
Alfinger, Ambrose, 165
Algonquin Indians, 164-165
Almagest, Ptolemy, 18
Al-Sufi, drawing by, *18
Amazon River, *map* 105, *110-115; origin of name, 111; Spanish expedition, 105, *108-115
American Indians, 19-20, 83, *108, 111, *134-135, 164-165; Alaska, *158; Brazil, 19, 83, 165, 166, 167; Columbus' encounters with, 55, 58, 83; conversion of, 167; domination or extermination of, 19-20, 164-165, *176-177; Magellan's encounters with, 83, 97-98; North American, 19, 102, *128-129, 130, *131-133, 164-165; Verrazano's encounter with, 101; West Indies, 19, 55, 164. *See also* Aztec empire; Inca empire; Maya
Americas: Columbus' discoveries, *12-13, 51, *maps* 53-54, 55, 58, 59-60; Drake on Pacific coast, 84, *map* 138, 139-140; mapping of, *map* 64, 65, *maps* 68-71, 95, 98, 99, 101, *map* 105, *map* 127; origin of name, 96; post-Columbian discoveries, 51-52, *map* 53; problems of exploration of, 95; recognized as new continent, 96, 100, 101; trade with, 41, 170. *See also* Central America; North America; South America; West Indies
Amsterdam, 118
Amundsen, Roald, 126
Andes, *106-107; crossed by Spanish expeditions, 105-108

Anian, Strait of, 120, 122, 123, 140
Animals, observation and depiction of, *130, *149, *153-155, *158, 164, *165
Antarctic Ocean, Cook in, 146
Antarctica, 146, 154
Anthropology, beginnings of, 166-167, 168
Anticosti Island, discovery of, 101
Antilles Islands, 51, 79; on Cantino chart, *map* 64; Columbus in, 58
Antipodes, 33
Antwerp, 170
Arab dhow, 14
Arab scholarship, 18, 118
Arab trade, 18, 37. *See also* Moslems
Arabian Sea: Portuguese trade monopoly, 102; trade route, *map* 37
Arawak Taino Indians, 19, 55, 164, 166
Archangel, English trade at, 119, 123
Arctic Ocean, navigability of, *map* 121
Arctic voyages, 16, 25, *116, 117-126. *See also* Northeast passage; Northwest passage
Arizona, Coronado in, 105
Arts: dealers, *46-47; Dutch painting, *10, *39-45, 46; native, *144, *162, *171-181
Asia: on Cantino chart, *map* 64-65; Columbus' belief in having reached, 52, 55, 56, 58, 59; European medieval ideas of, 31-32, *33; exploration of hinterland, 102-103, 104; first realization of westward distance from Europe, 96-97; Marco Polo in, 12, 32, 52, 56, *103; missionaries in, 167-168; northern coast, misconceptions, 118, 123; in Ptolemy's world, *map* 62; on Renaissance maps, *64-65, *70-71, 95; search for Atlantic route to, 52-53, *map* 54, 55, 96, *map* 97, 98, 100-101; search for northern passage to, 16, 25, 79, 101-102, *116, 117-120, *map* 121, 122-126; 13th Century European travelers in, 11-12, 32
Astrolabes, *72, 75, 90, *91
Astronomy: of antiquity, 62, 66; Arab, *18; Ptolemy, *63; Renaissance, 19, 62, *66-67. *See also* Celestial navigation
Atlantic Ocean: on Cantino chart, *map* 64; Columbus' expeditions, 28, *maps* 53-54, 55-56, 57-60; on 15th Century maps, 22, 51, *62-63; fogs, *26-27; islands, *map* 8, 33, 51; on medieval maps, 31; Portuguese-Spanish demarcation lines, *map* 57, *map* 64, 65, 96; post-Columbian expeditions across, 95-96, *map* 97, 99-102; pre-Columbian expeditions across, 12, 14, 51-52, *map* 53, 99; on 16th Century maps, *64, *68-71; trade and ports, *40-41, 170; wind and traffic patterns, 18, *map* 53, 55, 79
Atlantis, 51
Australia, *map* 138, 143; absent on 1527 map, 69; Cook in, 145, 148, *153; dis-

covery of, 141; exploration of coast of, 141-142, 145; Great Barrier Reef, 143, 145; west coast of, dangers of navigation, 27
Azores Islands, 33, *map* 57, 100; Columbus in, *map* 54, 55; storms, 27; year of discovery, 51
Aztec empire, 11, 19-20, 60, 100; codices, *176-177

B

Backstaff, *78
Baffin, William, 126
Baffin Bay, 126; Davis in, *map* 121, 124
Baffin Island, 51, *map* 121, 122; mapping of, 126
Bahama Islands, Columbus in, *12-13, *map* 54, 55
Bahía Cortés, 58
Bahrein, Persian Gulf, 102
Balboa, Vasco Nuñez de, 96-97, 100
Banks Islands, Pacific, discovery of, 141
Bantam, Java, 141
Baré, Jeanne, 143
Barents, Willem, expedition of, 16, *116, 117, *map* 121, *125, 126
Barents Sea, 120, *map* 121
Batavia, Java, 48, *map* 138, 142
Bear Island, *map* 121
Belalcázar, Sebastián de, 99
Belén, early settlement of, 59
Benin, bronze plaque from, *174
Bengal, Bay of, trade, 104
Bering Strait, Cook in, 156
Berlin, in 16th Century, 100
Berrio, the, 36
Beyeren, Abraham van, painting by, *42
Biscay, Bay of, 74, 75
Blaeu, Willem, map by, *70-71
Boothia, Gulf of, 126
Borneo, *map* 138
Boswell, James, quoted, 146
Bougainville, Louis Antoine de, 143, 145
Bramante, Donato, 100
Brazil, 80, 137; Cabral's discovery of, 96, *map* 97, 102; Dutch trade *40-41; exploration of coast of, 95, 96, *map* 97; Indians of, 19, 83, 165, 166, 167; Magellan in, 83, 97; mapping of coast, *map* 64, 65, 95, 96; missionaries in, 167; Portuguese claim to, *map* 57; slavery in, 166
Bray, Jan de, painting by, *39
Bristol, 118
British Empire, first use of phrase, 139
Brueghel, Pieter, painting by, *10
Bry, Theodor de, engravings by, *30, *94
Buddhism, 167
Bull *Aeterni regis*, line of, *map* 57
Bull *Inter caetera*, line of, *map* 57
Burma, trade, 104
Burrough, Stephen, 122, 123; expedition of, 119-120, *map* 121

C

Cabo da Volta, Southwest Africa, *map* 37
Cabot, John, 99, 117; North American expeditions of, *map* 97, 99-100
Cabot, Sebastián, 15, 80, 83, 100, 118, 119, 122, 123
Cabral, Pedro Alvares, 83, 166; expedition of, 95-96, *map* 97, 102
Cacafuego, the, 140
Cadamosto, Alvise da, 34, 83
Cairo, 36, *map* 37
Calicut, India, *map* 37; Cabral in, 102; Covilhã in, 35; Da Gama in, 37-38, 162

California, believed an island, 140
Callao, Peru, *map* 138, 140
Cambodia, trade, 104
Caminha, Pedro Vaz de, 166, 168
Camões, Luis Vaz de, 170
Canada: coastal exploration, 75; French exploration of coast of, *map* 97, 101-102; search for northwest passage around, 25, 27, 101-102, *map* 121, 122-123, 124-126
Canary Islands, 33, *map* 37, 52, 56, *map* 57, 79; Columbus in, 53, *map* 54; year of discovery, 51
Cannibalism, 15, 58, 166
Cantino, Alberto, 79
Cantino chart, *64-65, 79
Canton, China, 20
Cão, Diogo, expedition of, 34-35, *map* 37
Cap Haitien, 55, 58
Cape Agulhas, 36
Cape Blanco, 33
Cape Bojador, 33, 34
Cape Breton, 101
Cape Cod, 52
Cape Cross, 34, 35, *map* 37
Cape de San Francisco, 140
Cape Hatteras, 101
Cape Horn, 27, 74, 148
Cape Nun, 33
Cape of Good Hope, 27, 69, 75, 79, 166; first roundings of, 35, 36, *map* 37
Cape Pilar, 98
Cape St. Catherine, 35, *map* 37
Cape São Roque, 96
Cape Tabin, 118, 124
Cape Town, 36
Cape Verde, 33, *map* 57
Cape Verde Islands, *map* 37, *map* 54, 80; discovery of, 75
Cape York, 142, 145, 146
Caravels, 36, 53
Caribbean: Columbus in, *12-13, *map* 54, 55, 58, 59, 60; exploration of coastline, 96; flora of, 58, *132, *133; Indians of, 55, 58, 83; Spanish conquest, 105
Carletti, Francesco, 166-167
Carlsen, Elling, 126
Carpentaria, Gulf of, *map* 138, 141, 142
Carpini, Giovanni de Plano, 12
Carrack, *87, *88-89
Carte Pisane, chart, *77
Carteret, Alexander, 142, 143
Cartier, Jacques, 75; expeditions of, *map* 97, 101-102
Cartography, 18, 31, *61-71. *See also* Maps and mapping
Carvel-built vessels, *86
Cathay, *map* 9, 20, 52, *103; Columbus' belief in having reached, 55, 56, 57, 96, 100; Goes' overland expedition to, 102, 104; identified with China, 104; John Cabot's belief in having reached, 100; search for eastbound route to, 95; search for northern route to, 101-102, *116, 117-126; search for westbound route to, 52-55, 58, 95, 96-98, 100-101
Cebu, Magellan in, 98
Cecil, William, 57
Celebes, *map* 138
Celestial charts, *66-67
Celestial globe, *63
Celestial navigation, *68, 75, 76, 77, *78, 90, *91; and fog, 27
Central America: discovery by Columbus, *map* 54, 59; exploration of coast of, 75, 96; first European settlement in, 59; Spanish conquest of, 19-20, 96-97, 105
Ceuta, Portuguese capture of, 32
Ceylon, Portuguese in, 102
Chaleur Bay, discovery of, 101
Chanca, Dr., 58
Chancellor, Richard, 119, 121; quoted, 162-163
Charles I, King of Spain. *See* Charles V

PRINTED IN U.S.A.

XXXXXX